scm centrebooks

John Gray

What about the Children?

SCM PRESS LTD

334 01769 6

First published 1970
by SCM Press Ltd
56 Bloomsbury Street London WC1

© *SCM Press Ltd 1970*

Printed in Great Britain by
Billing & Sons Limited
Guildford and London

Contents

Acknowledgements

The author and publisher of this book would like to express the following grateful acknowledgements: to Chatto and Windus Ltd for permission to use an extract from Chapter 1 of Iris Murdoch's *The Red and the Green*; to Gerald Duckworth and Co. Ltd for the passage from 'Moor Park' by Caroline Grosvenor, included in Susan Tweedsmuir's reminiscences *The Lilac and the Rose* (Duckworth, 1952); and to Laurence Pollinger Limited and to the Estate of the late Mrs Frieda Lawrence for permission to use an extract from *The Rainbow* by D. H. Lawrence, published by William Heinemann Ltd.

Preface

What about the children? A book with so general a title, in a series where the other titles are rather more particular and precise, must explain its purpose at the start and acquaint its readers with what to expect. This book is, in fact, concerned with the children of Christians, their place in the church and all the questions which this can raise in today's world. Naturally, what it has to say will be more relevant in some countries than in others, and more applicable to some branches of the church than to others, but this is inevitable in any writing in a field so vast and complicated.

The attitude of the Christian church towards its children over the centuries is a notable part of this complication. A strong belief that children belong within the fellowship of the church has been often accompanied by a curious reservation that they do not *quite* belong. The result has been a kind of schizophrenic attitude towards them, which numerous attempts have been made to overcome. Sometimes they have been treated as adults, as if adults alone were of the kingdom of heaven, in spite of Jesus' saying about children and the kingdom. They have been assumed capable of prodigious intellectual apprehension of the truths of religion, and of momentous decisions. Yet at other times they have been treated as babes, incapable of even the simplest learning or the most elementary response. They have been continually seen, but only seldom heard and accepted in their own right.

There is much to be learned from the history of the church's treatment of children, both as example and as warning. But perhaps even more necessary is a return to first principles and a reconsideration of the whole matter. Fortunately, there are at last encouraging signs that a new look is not only becoming possible, but is also actively being investigated. The work of theologians on the one hand, and sociologists, psychologists, educationalists on the other may be able to bring a new perspective to the question of children and Christian upbringing.

First, the theologians. Two recent discussions are of special importance. On the one hand, much interest has been displayed by all the churches in the doctrine of baptism. Any such study is bound to have repercussions on attitudes to children and the programmes to be used with them. A report produced by the World Council of Churches, entitled *One Lord, One Baptism*, argued that more consideration of the meaning of baptism and what it conveyed would give clearer content and a new dimension to preaching and teaching:

> The more the baptized learn to see their whole life in the light of their baptism, the more does their life take on the pattern of life in Christ.[1]

On the other hand, the revived interest in the Bible and theology seems to demand not only an educated ministry but an educated laity as well. To plan such lay education would also mean fresh consideration of what should be taught to the church's children if they were to grow up literate in the things of the faith. So churches began to realize again that teaching was of the very essence of the church, and ceased to apologize for asking that children should be instructed. There was general agreement that:

> It belongs to the fundamental nature of Christian instruction to impart to the learner a good deal of information which he does not

know and could not acquire apart from receiving it from without and from others.[2]

It is good that these two insights should be appearing at the same time, because one corrects an attitude which can equate Christian upbringing with intellectualism, and the other corrects an attitude which can equate it with sacramentalism. Such thinking, too, has revived theological interest in an area from which the theologians seemed to have withdrawn at the point when catechisms went out of favour and children's upbringing in the church fell under the spell of the discoveries of child psychology.

These latter discoveries are not, however, to be regarded as aberrations or as irrelevant to what Christians seek to do for and with children. For at least they have exploded the myth that the child is a young adult, and have created a new awareness of the importance of children's interests and needs as factors in their learning and understanding, if not necessarily the only ones. Moreover, the most recent developments have been researches into religious education as a special field, and in particular into children's thinking.[3]

Some of these new studies are extremely controversial. There may not be general agreement about the validity of the research methods employed or the complete reliability of all the results, but they have shifted attention from the learning to the learner in a quite salutary way. Anyone who is concerned with how the church deals with children will have to question both presuppositions and procedures in the light of the new information available.

A second avenue of development in this direction may come from the application of sociology to religious education, as it has already come to be applied to general education. Again, a recent writer in the field of Christian education has argued that an important clue in developing models for the communication of faith has been offered by

11

social scientists who study culture and the process by which a society hands on its beliefs to succeeding generations.[4]

Now thinking cannot be divorced from happening, and the happening of our time which most affects the theme with which we are concerned is the rise of the modern secular society. Many definitions have been offered of this new situation. Kathleen Nott succinctly remarks that what has happened is:

> The withdrawal of areas of thought and life from religious – and finally also from metaphysical – control, and the attempt to understand and live in these areas in the terms which they alone offer.[5]

Thus the church can no longer expect children to be culturally conditioned to at least its values as they are conventionally understood. Nor may it much longer be able to find in the state schools a religious education, largely Bible-based and centred on Christianity, as has been the tradition in a number of countries. The effect of this must be to make Christians enquire how much they have in the past depended on society to supply elements of upbringing which in the earliest days of the church had to be supplied by the church itself, against formidable outside pressure. Churches in countries without provision for religious education in state schools have more experience of this situation, and may have something to teach others who have not yet come to realize what it means.

A last factor, and by no means least, is the new status of youth in highly developed societies where their taste, their fashion, their music and their amusements are all specially catered for. Maturity seems to come quicker, and tutelage and authoritarian attitudes are resented. In this new young world, church congregations seem to grow older. Much of church youth work, apart from a few conspicuous success stories, is in considerable disarray. Analysis of loss and drift suggests that the church is keeping less and less children within its sphere of influence for less time. Of course, some have always gone away in the strain of adolescence, which can lead to doubt as well as faith; and some of them who went away have come back again to full and active membership. Nevertheless, it is no time for complacency and excuses that 'things have always been like this'. For the loss and drift is far from being materialistic and self-interested. Many young people are showing a commitment to sacrificial living and a concern for the underprivileged according to the best insights of Christianity while denying any Christian motivation and rejecting the church itself. Their concern often puts conventional Christianity to shame.

All these factors, both positive and negative, may make this book timely if it can offer some practical help. Christians seem far from sure what responsibility should belong to parents, what to schools and what to the church; outsiders, disturbed about the dangers of an open society and anxious not to leave children without any guidance at all, may well be ready to give a hearing to a re-expressed Christian point of view.

NOTES

1. *One Lord, One Baptism*, WCC Report, London 1960, p. 71.
2. T. F. Torrance, *The School of Faith*, London 1959, p. xxvii.
3. See especially Ronald Goldman, *Religious Thinking from Childhood to Adolescence*, London 1964.
4. C. E. Nelson, *Where Faith Begins*, Richmond, Virginia 1967, p. 35.
5. Quoted in M. Jarrett-Kerr, *The Secular Promise*, London 1964, p. 25.

1 Some Basic Ideas

What is 'Christian nurture'?

Even in apparently simple subjects, Christian writers seem prone to introducing technical terms, sometimes of frightening complexity. To some degree this happens even when they are talking about children. So it will be well to look at one particular phrase right at the start, 'Christian nurture'. This rather old-fashioned term is used quite regularly to cover the whole range of activities through which the Christian church expresses concern for the children within its fold. A particular term like this has its advantages, because at least it makes us stop and think before going beyond it, and brings us face to face with a number of basic questions.

'Christian nurture' is not easy to define briefly. Attempts to produce tidy definitions usually fail, because they lean too heavily upon descriptions of nurture in general or, at the other extreme, on what has been wittily called 'boyhood recollected in theology'.[1] In use the term appears to be wider than 'religious education', or even 'Christian education', both of which are used of other than church situations. At the same time, it always seems to mean more than the specifically church activities with which it tends to be associated, like Sunday schools or confirmation classes. So perhaps a more roundabout approach will shed more light on it.

In his study of religious language, the Bishop of Durham,

Ian Ramsey, made a useful distinction between 'models' and 'qualifiers'. A 'model', he suggested, is a situation with which we are all familiar, and which can be used for reaching another situation with which we are not so familiar; one which, without the model, we should not recognize so easily. A 'qualifier' is a directive which prescribes a special way of developing these 'model' situations. If we apply this approach to the phrase 'Christian nurture', then the model would be what is implied by the word 'nurture', and the qualifier whatever is meant by the adjective 'Christian'.[2] How does this work out?

The meaning of 'nurture' is simple enough. The *Concise Oxford Dictionary* defines it as 'bringing up, training, fostering care'. Nurture, then, as a human activity, will cover what parents and teachers and society and the state seek to do with and for children. It will obviously apply to a variety of operations – feeding and clothing; training in elementary hygiene and cultivation of good habits; introduction to standards of conduct, taste and value; initiation into the ethos of the particular society. As a human process, at least in the case of normal children, it should have an end, and the over-prolongation of any aspect beyond its proper time can transform a good to an evil. A mother's tender care for a young child is excellent, but for a young man to be tied to his mother's apron strings is undesirable, and nurture gone bad. So there should be progression in nurture towards some kind of independence and personal responsibility.

What then does the qualifier 'Christian' add to this description, or how does it alter it? Obviously there must be common ground and some common purpose between Christian nurture and nurture not so precisely defined. One cannot imagine, for example, a situation where Christian parents would be indifferent to the feeding or the clothing of their children, or the Christian church either, in those cases where the children have no one to care for them. When we read in the Epistle of James that, 'Religion that is pure and undefiled before God is this: to visit orphans or widows in their affliction' (1.27), it is difficult to believe that the writer is thinking that the visitor will only bring good words and not the more practical things which the orphans will need.

There have, however, been times when Christians, because of what they believe, had to consider whether to feed and clothe their children differently from other children in the same society. We can imagine the people to whom Paul wrote at Corinth wondering whether it was right to give their children 'meat offered to idols'; we can imagine the Quaker Robert Barclay wondering how to explain to children in his connection that 'it is not lawful for a Christian to use superfluities in apparel as are of no use, save for ornament and vanity'.[3]

Again, it is hard to think that Christian parents would wish to deny their children education. But there have been times when they have wanted to lay down special conditions about the schooling of their children and about the curriculum to be offered to them in school. There has seldom come from the Christian church any widespread objection to education as such, and even Tertullian, the passionate second-century Christian controversialist who often seemed so against, is driven, as he says himself, to 'look into the necessity of a literary education' and to recognize that 'it can be partly allowed'.[4] When the church founded its own schools, education was not confined to religious education, although it naturally did always include it. Similarly, parents who were not Christian have also expressed desires about the kind of schooling they thought best for their children, and have sometimes objected to what has been offered them. This attitude is vigorously upheld at the present time.

It therefore appears that Christian nurture both resembles and differs from ordinary human nurture in discernible ways which can at times be illustrated by historical examples. Where it differs, this is because Christian nurture appears to be subject to a different control, normative for the whole process and so influencing particular instances of common nurture along new lines. But what is the nature of this control? How can we specify more precisely the way in which Christian nurture differs from ordinary human nurture? Answering these questions is clearly most important, for upon the answers to them will depend our views of the way in which Christian nurture is to be carried out in practice.

The biblical basis

As ever, the place to begin our investigation would seem to be the Bible. The word 'nurture' occurs in the Authorized Version just once, in Ephesians 6.4, where fathers are exhorted not to provoke their children to wrath but to 'bring them up in the nurture and admonition of the Lord'. This phraseology is reflected in many baptismal liturgies and has also found its way into the introduction to the Anglican marriage service. The original passage therefore offers a convenient starting place for uncovering the distinctive nature of Christian nurture.

First, it should be noted that the Greek word for 'bring up' is a neutral word, which pagans as well as Christians could employ to describe their own efforts on behalf of their children. The new and apparently special thing that the fathers of Ephesus are urged to do is 'to bring them up *in the nurture and admonition of the Lord*'. This simple phrase is not as easy as it looks. It could have two meanings here, and although the two meanings overlap, it is important to discover the one which is more in harmony with the main trend of New Testament thought. That is, we must also take into consideration other ideas which, while not seeming to refer to this precise context, bear upon it and point in the direction of the likeliest interpretation.

The first possible meaning might lay principal stress on the parents. They are to be the agents of religious instruction, presumably setting before their children the story of Jesus and his love and his example and the precepts of the church to follow. 'Of the Lord' is purely objective, so to speak the subject-matter that they are to come to know. On the other hand, 'of the Lord' might be the most important part of the sentence. This is the second possible meaning. The sentence could be understood to say that it is the Lord who is the principal agent in nurture and admonition, that Christian nurture is a divine action in which the parents most certainly have a share, but which neither originates from them nor is completed by them. This second meaning obviously includes the first, and at the same time adds a whole other dimension to it. Such a suggestion may seem quite alien to the mid-twentieth century, but it should certainly not be left out of consideration altogether.

This second meaning is illuminated and clarified by two great images of the church which appear in the New Testament. In Romans 11.17 ff., Paul has a famous picture of the olive tree, from which some branches are broken off and to which others are grafted in their place to share the richness of the olive tree; in John 15, Jesus is made to speak of himself as the true vine: 'As the branch cannot bear fruit by itself, unless it abides in the vine, neither can you, unless you abide in me.' Both these passages are concerned with growth and fruit producing, an imagery which is appropriate to nurture. In Paul, growth comes from being 'grafted in'; this, too, has had its effect on baptismal services with their emphasis on being 'grafted' or 'engrafted' into Christ. In John, growth can only come because the branches are 'in Christ', who is the vine.

Now if these images are applied to our thinking about Christian nurture, they confirm what was hinted at above, that such nurture is not a human action to make believers' children Christian. Rather, it is to be seen as something that God has done or will continue to do. As John Baillie writes:

> When a child is born and baptized into the household of faith, and acquiesces in the manner of his upbringing, the disposition of faith, operating through his Christian home, is already being found in him.[5]

Such a child is already a Christian appropriate to his age and development and not to be made one by any human process. 'If the root is holy,' says St Paul, 'so are the branches . . . It is not you that support the root but the root that supports you.'

Christian nurture, then, means the nurture of Christ. It begins with the birth of a child into the family of God, is signed and sealed in his baptism and is acknowledged when that baptism is accepted and confirmed.

The human contribution

There is, however, a real danger in this description if it is left here without any further comment or reservation. For it might leave the impression that what we have been saying is no more than a translation into religious terms of the secular arguments about the influence of heredity and environment. This has indeed been one of the main criticisms offered against such an approach.[6] Moreover, a description along these lines can suggest that the nurture

20

of Christ is an invincible, divine process apart from all human helps, leaving no room for human freedom and human choice, and overriding all human failings. That would make it resemble in theological terms some of the cruder theories of baptismal regeneration.

If we look at the portraits of Jesus offered in the Gospels, however, we can see that this is certainly not a way characteristic of him. A close examination of the two images of the olive and the vine also offers additional correction. In the image of the vine from the Gospel of John, the branches must remain in the vine before there can be any fruit. This implies what has been called 'a mutual abiding',[7] with the possibilities of withdrawal and falling away. Indeed, the image itself is strained, because John is describing the relation of Christ to the members of his church, and this cannot be covered without remainder in a horticultural image. Similarly Paul takes care to stress the freedom of the branches in his picture of the olive tree, thus straining that image even further: 'They were broken off because of their unbelief, but you stand fast only through faith' (Rom. 2.20).

If such qualifications are not made, it is easy to understand the difficulties which those who stand for Believer's Baptism find in Infant Baptism, when it is understood as conveying all the benefits of Christ in an *ex opere operato* fashion. To adopt such an attitude would, of course, also be to misunderstand what is claimed here for Christian nurture as the nurture of Christ. It must be acknowledged quite openly that the church has never so miserably failed its children as when it baptized them and left them to their own devices. An introduction to an old catechism has this to say to its readers:

A greater regard is to be had to your Children and Servants than to your Cattel, yet generally there is no more heed. Ye lift your

21

children in the Roll of the Church and then permit them to follow their own ways without precept or example.

It is significant that the passage from the Epistle to the Ephesians examined above is directed to parents. It does not say, 'Leave your children; for the Lord will nurture and teach them'; it sees a place for the parents' co-operation in encouraging and fostering and shepherding the young into the full possession of that nurture which the Lord always supplies. The Larger Catechism emphasizes the necessary part to be played by the baptized themselves:

The needful but neglected duty of improving our baptism is to be performed by us all our life long.

It will involve 'growing up', 'endeavouring'.[8]

The work of Christ

Nurture, then, is the interaction between Christ and the children born into his church. We have dealt with one objection to the argument that we have outlined, that by putting emphasis on the part played by Christ, nurture might seem to be an automatic process, divorced from the activity of human agents. But there is a second argument to be coped with, this time from almost the opposite pole. Do not such attempts at the description of Christian nurture which have so far been made tend to appear 'allegorical and mystical'?[9] What, in the time at which we are living, can be meant by 'the part played by Christ'?

No short answer can be given to either the objection or the question. For to answer it requires a presentation of the whole of Christian belief. All that can be said here is that if Christianity demands, as it does, a constituent not located exclusively in experience, in the social context, if it is based on a belief in the action of God in his world and particularly in Christ, then for Christian parents, the belief that Christ can work in their children should be none the less real than any other article of faith. This does not imply that such an activity does not touch on other children or work in them in other situations than in the church. It merely says that there is a special constituency to which Christ is related in a special way, the church. Here, of course, we come up against the whole mystery of particularity, of election, both of the Old Israel and the New Israel. It goes without saying that this election should be understood as positive election to serve, and in no other way.

We might take the argument one stage further, to a final point, by considering one more image of the church in the New Testament: Paul's image of the church as the body of Christ. Here again, the image suggests rather than covers the distinctiveness of the idea that the nurture of the Lord is the nurture of the members, both at the same time, and the one dependent upon the other. A modern writer has tried to put this difficult thought into his own words:

> It is an action of the church, performed upon its members and upon those who may become members, which is similar to a body extending itself by adding new parts. It is also similar to a body doing something to its members which makes them more completely members than they were before.[10]

But this action is controlled by the head and at every point furthered by him, and is directed towards the coming of age which is seen as a necessary part of ordinary human nurture. Ephesians 4 uses this image of the body to describe a growth to maturity which requires the exercise of specially given gifts by human agents, yet in the whole process Christ is at work:[11]

> And these were his gifts: some to be apostles, some prophets, some evangelists, some pastors and teachers, to equip God's people for work in his service, to the building up of the body of Christ. So shall we all at last attain to the unity inherent in our faith and

knowledge of the Son of God; to mature manhood, measured by nothing less than the full stature of Christ. We are no longer to be children, tossed by the waves and whirled about by every fresh gust of teaching, dupes of rogues and their deceitful schemes. No, let us speak the truth in love; so shall we fully grow up into Christ. He is the head, and on him the whole body depends. Bonded and bound together in every constituent joint, the whole process grows through the due activity of each part and builds itself up in love (Eph. 4.11–16, NEB).

In a single sentence, at the opening of his famous book *Christian Nurture*, Horace Bushnell sums up the whole argument of this chapter:

There is some kind of nurture which is of the Lord, deriving a quality and power from him.[12]

NOTES

1. William Barclay, *Educational Ideals in the Ancient World*, London 1959, p. 253.

2. Ian T. Ramsey, *Religious Language*, London 1957, pp. 61 f.

3. Robert Barclay, *An Apology for the True Christian Divinity*, Quoted in Waldo Beach and H. Richard Niebuhr, (eds.), *Christian Ethics*, New York 1955, p. 320.

4. S. L. Greenslade (ed.), *Early Latin Theology*, Library of Christian Classics, vol. 5, London 1956, pp. 92 f.

5. John Baillie, *Baptism and Conversion*, London 1964, p. 47.

6. E.g. Horace Bushnell's *Christian Nurture*, Yale 1947, has been so criticized.

7. Paul S. Minear, *Images of the Church in the New Testament*, London 1961, p. 42.

8. T. F. Torrance, *The School of Faith*, London 1959, p. 225.

9. J. D. Butler, *Religious Education: The Foundation and Practice of Nurture*, New York 1962, p. 21

10. Butler, *op. cit.*, p. 20.

11. See also an interesting discussion in Donald Baillie, *Theology of the Sacraments*, London 1957, pp. 86 f.

12. Bushnell, *op. cit.*, p. 3.

2 Some Basic Ingredients

The Greek word used in Ephesians 6.4, the passage which formed the basis of the previous chapter, for nurture is *paideia*. It was

> one of the most important and meaning-filled words in the Greek world. Its earliest meaning was simply, child-rearing. Its later and more typical meaning in Greek literature, becoming almost a technical term, was that which you did to produce the ideal man of Hellenic times, which was the man of *arete* or virtue.[1]

The *paideia* of the Lord has its own special objective: 'Mature manhood measured by nothing less than the full stature of Christ' (Eph. 4.13). Therefore, like its classical counterpart, it requires its own distinctive curriculum. Parents and teachers and the church itself, as we have seen, are not only channels for what the Lord supplies, but also conscious co-operators in the process. Thus Luther calls parents 'apostles and prophets', because they teach the Gospel. This conscious activity, like all education, must have some programme from which to work.

This programme will be regarded by those who operate it as a 'given' – and once again we must pause briefly to look at terminology. 'Given' is a useful term, not least because of the obvious implications it has of something quite apart from the recipient. It is, of course, the English form of the more familiar Latin word *datum*, *data*. It can be best understood by a rather formal definition:

> The given of any discipline is its subject-matter, what it is all about . . . basically something imposed upon us and not of our devising; it is, too, the premises from which all our investigation flows; with its problems and enquiries it sustains our curiosity and it provides the contextual framework within which the whole discipline moves.[2]

The question is, is it possible to speak in such terms of a given curriculum for Christian nurture? Is there a programme which preserves the objectivity of what is offered and yet implies response and creativity (as well as questioning) on the part of those who will use it and those with whom it will be used? Further, is it possible to separate out the main elements of such a curriculum and to ask whether they will apply to all places and all times? These are the issues which are now raised, and an attempt will be made to deal with them in a positive way.

The Bible

First, in any programme of Christian nurture, the Bible deserves to be considered as part of the 'given' as we have just outlined it. Indeed, one early Christian writer seems to refer to the Bible as the *paideia* of God. Historically, it seems to have had this place in the Christian church from the beginning.

It is not surprising that this should have happened. For the church drew on Judaism before it made contact with the wider Greek world, and the Jew was well aware of the need to familiarize the children with all the words of the Law. This was not their human law, but God's Law, symbolized by the story of Moses receiving the two tablets on Mount Sinai.

Deuteronomy 6.4–9 is the Jewish confession of faith – to be said every morning and every evening by faithful Jews. It runs:

> Listen, Israel: Yahweh our God is the one Yahweh. You shall love Yahweh your God with all your heart, with all your soul, with all your strength. Let these words I urge on you today be written on your heart. You shall repeat them to your children . . . (*Jerusalem Bible*).

Jewish parents, then, were not likely to forget their responsibility for the religious nurture of their children and for their introduction to the knowledge of God's law. So Josephus, the Jewish historian, who was roughly a contemporary of Jesus' disciples, has this to say in defence of the laws and customs of the Jewish people:

> It also commands us to bring up those children in learning and to exercise them in the laws and make them acquainted with the acts of their predecessors in order to their imitation of them and that they might be nourished up in the laws from their infancy and might neither transgress them nor have any pretence for their ignorance of them.[3]

By this is surely implied that familiarity with the Bible would be a normal requirement for Jewish parents to secure for their children, and that the same would then most likely become normative for the Gentiles within the church when they came to deal with their own children. For such Gentiles would have to learn the Bible for themselves, and obviously did so, as Paul's Old Testament references in his letters reveal. That knowledge, then, they would share with their own children on the Jewish model.

II Timothy 3.15 remarks how Timothy has from childhood been 'acquainted with the sacred writings which are able to instruct you for salvation through faith in Christ Jesus'; 'the sacred writings' must at least include Scripture, even if it means more. The same passage continues:

> All scripture is inspired by God and profitable for teaching, for reproof, for correction, and for training in righteousness, that the man of God may be complete, equipped in every good work. (II Tim. 3.16 f.)

With the word 'training' we are back to the Greek word *paideia*.

Werner Jaeger tells of Gregory of Nyssa that when he quotes Scripture as the supreme authority,

> instead of saying 'the prophet says' or 'Christ says' as would be most natural for us, he writes innumerable times, 'the prophet Isaiah educates us', or 'the Apostle educates us' (*paideuei*), implying that what the Bible teaches must be accepted as the *paideia* of the Christian.[4]

The Reformation made the same point in its own way with its insistence on providing men with the Bible in their own tongue and giving children the ability to read that they might be able to read it for themselves. Only seldom has the insistence on the Bible been at the expense of other literature and learning, but its peculiar place has always been recognized, and with that the distinctive need for the children to be schooled in it.

The importance of the Bible in past nurture is, then, clear enough. But is the Bible still essential today? To judge from the practice of the churches in worship, in church schools and in Sunday schools, the question is to be answered with a resounding 'Yes'. The tradition is still very strong, for behind the tradition lies the fact that most churches in their standards admit the place and importance of the Bible. Difficulties, however, about its nature and use are there. The main theological difficulty seems to lie in how the Bible is to be interpreted. For some, indeed, this difficulty is so great that they object to the Bible as outmoded:

> The Bible may well embody a revelation of the Word, but men have long since lost any certain or sure means of interpreting its meaning as revelation.[5]

Less radical, but no less important, are the pleas of Christians who, on psychological and educational grounds, plead for a reconsideration of the ways in which the Bible is to be mediated to children and who produce as evidence the confusion and misunderstanding which can be the result of misguided zeal or what Goldman calls the 'they must know the Bible argument'.[6]

These objections may be noted, and the whole question of children and the Bible will be considered in a later chapter. But despite them, the majority of Christians would still seem to agree that the Bible remains a necessary element in the upbringing which they believe God has provided for their children. Above all, the words of Jesus about the Scriptures in the Gospel of John still have considerable force: 'Their testimony points to me' (John 5.39 NEB). Perhaps the church has not always used this part of its curriculum wisely or well with the children in its charge. At times the connection between Christ and Scripture has been so made as to obscure the testimony of the scriptures to Christ and even to hinder children growing up into him. Perhaps a new understanding of Scripture and children, such as seems to be developing in our own time, will lead to new methods for this part of the curriculum. At any rate, perhaps we may claim Scripture here as 'given' for any curriculum for children growing up within the church.

'The means of grace'

A second 'given' is harder to define. It covers that whole area which has traditionally been included in the phrase 'the means of grace'. The phrase is perhaps best defined in the answer to Question 154 in the Larger Catechism:

> The outward and ordinary means whereby Christ communicates to his church the benefits of his mediation and all his ordinances: especially the Word, Sacraments and Prayer, all of which are made effectual to the elect for their salvation.

It will be seen at once how this 'given' relates to the

previous section ('the Word'), but at the same time extends it into a new area. Here again in the beginning Christian parents might be expected to have proceeded on the Jewish model. The Jews already had in their sacred feasts and ceremonies what they regarded as ordinances provided by God, whereby they remembered and shared in his benefits. The children, too, would be taught to participate in the ordinances as they were able. A good example of this is the way in which the Mishnah of the Babylonian Talmud shows how the biblical injunction contained in Deuteronomy 6.20 ff. is fulfilled at the passover feast.

The Deuteronomy passage states the principle in general terms:

> When your son asks you in time to come, 'What is the meaning of the testimonies and the statutes and the ordinances which the Lord our God has commanded you?', then you shall say to your son, 'We were Pharaoh's slaves in Egypt; and the Lord brought us out of Egypt with a mighty hand; and the Lord showed signs and wonders, great and grievous, against Egypt and against Pharaoh and all his household, before our eyes; and he brought us out from there, that he might bring us in and give us the land which he swore to give to our fathers. And the Lord commanded us to do all these statutes, to fear the Lord our God, for our good always, that he might preserve us alive as at this day.'

A more specific form appears in the instructions for the passover:

> And when your children say to you, 'What is the meaning of this service?', you shall say, 'It is the sacrifice of the Lord's passover, for he passed over the houses of the people of Israel in Egypt, when he slew the Egyptians but spared our houses.' (Ex. 12.26 f.)

The passage from the Talmud reads as follows:

> They mix the second cup and here the son asks the father (and if the son has not enough understanding the father instructs him how to ask): 'Why is this night different from other nights? For on other nights we eat seasoned food once, but this night twice; on other nights we eat leavened or unleavened bread, but on this night, all is unleavened. On other nights we eat flesh, roast, stewed or cooked,

but this night, all is roast.' And according to the understanding of the son, his father instructs him. He begins with the disgrace and ends with the glory, and expands from 'A wandering Aramean was my father' until he finishes the whole section.[7]

In this way, the Jewish father helped his children to understand how great was the deliverance which they shared, just as if they had been in Egypt themselves and had themselves been set free.

Christians soon began to have their own special days and feasts: the Lord's Day and not the Sabbath, the Lord's Supper and Easter, and not the Jewish family meal and the Passover, and a whole system regulated the hours of the day and the keeping of the Christian year. Of course, this regulated life of devotion could become a burden as well as a blessing. Yet its basic principles were of obvious value to the parents who sought to introduce their children to the Christian faith and especially to Jesus, with whose birth, life, death and resurrection the chief events of the Christian year were associated and from whom they received their 'given' quality. One of the early church orders designed to regulate Christian liturgical and community life shows how even the hours for prayer are to be related to what happened to Christ. For example, 'at the third hour, pray then . . . for at that hour Christ was nailed to the Tree'.[8] It would be impossible to keep such hours of devotion and not learn about Jesus. It was only when the church went beyond this point and introduced excessive elaboration that the whole thing became too cumbersome and too difficult.

The Reformation represented a cutting back of this luxuriant development, but no one denied the need for children to be initiated into the worship of the church. The sharing of church worship was felt to be useful from an instructional point of view, as a remark of Luther's shows (here, as so often, he makes a good point by exaggeration):

> If such orders (i.e. liturgical orders) are necessary, it is specially because of simple-minded and young people who need to be and must be daily educated and trained in Scripture and the work of God so that they may become accustomed and skilled in it and fluent in it to the end that they may be able to be a witness to their faith and in turn lead others and help to further the reign of Christ. It is for this that we must read, sign, preach and write, and make prayers; and to promote this end – where it is necessary – I would have all the bells rung, have the organs played with all their pipes sounding, and everything resound that can resound.[9]

The Scots Reformers refused to entertain the Christian year, but they wished children to know 'the right form to pray unto God, the number, use and effects of the Sacraments'.

Worship would, from the beginning, include private prayer. Jesus' own example of private prayer and his teaching of a pattern prayer to his disciples (Luke 11.1–4; Matt. 6. 7–13) were there to be followed. So John Chrysostom writes in his work *The Right Way for Parents to Bring up Children:*

> Let him learn to pray and do not tell me that a lad would never conform to these practices . . . Let the boy be trained to pray . . . to keep vigils as much as he is able.

The Christian church clearly saw the relevance of all this to the Lord's purpose for his children, and it was surely right. But the same question now confronts us as before. Can the old methods now achieve the same results as they once did? Can regular practice of public worship or private prayer lead to Christian maturity in our modern society? Again, some theologians protest against liturgical worship and there is a strong movement concerned with the 'secularization' of prayer:

The church, its liturgies, creeds and confessions may well embody an epiphany of Christ, but that epiphany is distant from us and it cannot speak to our contemporary experience.[10]

Above all, there is protest from the children themselves. Surveys of their attitudes to Christianity have shown that whereas there is considerable interest in religious questions in general and Christianity in particular, the church is the great stumbling block. And by 'the church' is meant the church as found at worship on a Sunday morning or evening, engaged in its traditional form of services:

> The church is too old fashioned and set in its ways. The services are completely boring and moronic in the church I used to go to.

> The church service itself can be likened to a normal anatomical function like breathing. At first we can do it consciously, but soon it becomes automatic to do the same boring thing time after time, that one begins to do it unconsciously.[11]

Perhaps such objections are not so new as they sometimes seem. The following was written in *An Exhortation to Catechizing*, produced by the Provincial Assembly at London on 30 August 1655:

> Hence they have taken the boldness to describe the Scriptures as somewhat too dim, especially in comparison to their most glorious new light: to despise the Sacraments as if they were beggarly elements as the Jewish ceremonies: to deride the singing of Psalms as if David's harp were now out of tune; to reject prayer as if they had obtained to as plentiful a means of spiritual riches that it were a shame for them to crave any further supplies. And then, alas (think they), what should they vainly lose a seventh part of the year in the superstition of a weekly Sabbath, whereas their whole life is but one continued holy day? What should they defile themselves with the infectious airs of our corrupt church where we never assemble without constant confession of too many iniquities in our holy things? Shortly, what should they busy themselves too much in preparing themselves for heaven? We must know they are there already: nor can they acknowledge any other heaven besides that in their own bosom.

Those acquainted with 'worldly holiness' and 'God in the

depth' will be able to recognize the resemblances of old and new.

Again, new approaches are needed. The gap between worship and the world in which it is carried on must, if it exists, be bridged so that contemporary experience plays its proper part. Some attempt to suggest how this might be done will be made in another chapter. But the fact remains, that most Christians would still see worship and 'the means of grace' as a vital ingredient for the curriculum of God-given Christian nurture, where, perhaps more than anywhere else, the primacy of God's approach to man in Jesus Christ can be seen and apprehended.

The divine society

A third given is really the context of the other two, although here artificially separated from them for purposes of convenience. This is the divine society, the church of Jesus Christ in the world, where the Bible is interpreted and worship offered to God through Jesus Christ. This society should be observable in the midst of the larger society in which it is set, by its 'sacred' custom but equally through its 'secular' activities. Once again, we can see how this pattern developed from Judaism, and was taken over by the Christian church.

The training offered to the young in Judaism was training for life, and ultimately for life to be lived in widely differing surroundings and societies. It had to inculcate responsibilities towards the group of which the Jewish child formed a part and yet help towards a *modus vivendi*, where possible, with those who were outside this close fellowship. Good examples of such training appear in the early chapters of the Book of Daniel, which seeks to show through story the qualities which Jewish youths should display in a time of persecution. and the very different atmosphere and teaching of Ecclesiasticus, which seeks to apply the faith to a whole range of subjects, from how to behave at meals to the need to seek after wisdom.

Similarly, training in the Christian church had to be training for life, showing not only the obligation of Christians to fellow members but also the constant vocation to understand and perform God's will in the time and situation in which the church was set. The goal of the Christian was a manner of life worthy of the Lord, and entirely pleasing to him (Col. 1.10).[12]

As in Judaism, so too in Christianity, being a Christian in some forms of society could lead to the call to costly witness, at times in the extreme form of martyrdom. In a more favourable society, Christianity demanded a superlative citizenship and humanity of the kind that the first-century Apologists sought to claim as the characteristic of the Christians of their own day. There will always be such witness; for God never leaves himself without a witness, and some at least of the nature of this obedience and what it implies will be learned unconsciously through example. Tertullian gives an illuminating, if indirect, insight into what Christian obedience in his own time might imply, in his description of the plight of a Christian who marries a pagan husband:

> . . . if a station is to be kept, her husband will make an early appointment with her to go to the baths; if a fast is to be observed, her husband will, that very day, prepare a feast; if it be necessary to go out on an errand of Christian charity, never are duties at home more urgent! Who, indeed, would permit his wife to be taken from his side, when she is obliged to be present at evening devotions? Or, to take another example, who would not be concerned when she spends the whole night away from the house during the Paschal solemnities? Who, without feeling some suspicion, would let her go to assist at the Lord's Supper, when such vile rumours are spread about it? Who would suffer her to slip into prison to kiss the fetters of a martyr? Or, for that matter, to salute any one

of the brethren with a kiss? Who would allow her to wash the feet of the saints? To ply them with food and drink? Who would permit her to desire such things – or even to think of them? If one of the brethren, in travelling, stops at her house, what hospitality will he receive in the house of a pagan? If anyone is in need of assistance, the granary and pantry are closed and locked.[13]

Tertullian hardly sees how such a wife with such a husband can perform her 'Christian duties and devotions'. But there were obviously situations where she did, and even in such divided households, children would have set before them the example of an obedience which was not limited to the 'distinctive religious observances', but reached out to deeds of love in the common life. Augustine pays tribute to the witness shown by his own mother in such a household.[14]

However, example itself could not be enough without some help to people so that they could make their own decisions; so Christian literature from the Pauline epistles onwards has concerned itself with the kind of response which should be made by Christians in the common life of society to the demand which faith lays upon them. This may be the area which has most relevance to the question of the nature of Christian upbringing today.

It is not an area where the Christian past seems to have been able to give more to the present than a constant sense that Jesus is Lord, is to be obeyed. Sometimes the attempt to convey this has resulted in an entirely negative approach. Obedience to Christ has been presented to the children as consisting in keeping a whole system of rules and learning by casuistry how to extend them. The more positive approach, perhaps it is the more difficult, has been neglected, and the opportunity missed to help children to understand Christian obedience in terms of a creative response to ever-changing circumstances in the spirit of Christian love. The general result has been that many keep the churchly rules about worship and prayer, but abandon as hopeless the attempt to live as Christians in the world.

No one will doubt the value of this final part of the curriculum with its given reference to the will of God. Here we are brought up against the problem of the best way of teaching how to obey. That, too, will be investigated further in a later chapter.

From a historical point of view, the three elements we have been discussing, the Bible, the means of grace and the divine society seem to provide the core of the curriculum of Christian nurture. It remains to be seen whether the contemporary scene with all its problems will allow them to be pursued with new vigour and with the same degree of success. For we must not forget that it is a concentration on these elements which, allowing for all loss and failure, has caused sons to succeed fathers in the church from the very beginning down to our day. Are we likely to see a real break in the chain?

NOTES

1. Edward Farley, 'The Strange History of Christian *Paideia*', *Religious Education* LX, 1965, p. 5.

2. John McIntyre, *The Shape of Christology*, London 1966, p. 16.

3. *Josephus against Apion*, 2.27, translated by W. Whiston, London 1897, p. 552.

4. Werner Jaeger, *Early Christianity and Greek Paideia*, Harvard 1962, pp. 92 f.

5. Thomas Altizer, *The Gospel of Christian Atheism*, London 1967, p. 13.

6. Ronald Goldman, *Religious Thinking from Childhood to Adolescence*, p. 222.

7. Quoted by L. J. Sherrill, *The Rise of Christian Education*, New York 1950, p. 51.

8. See *The Apostolic Tradition of Hippolytus*, tr. B. S. Easton, Cambridge 1934, pp. 54 ff.

9. Luther, Preface to German Mass of 1526, quoted in J. J. von Allmen, *Worship: Its Theology and Practice*, London 1965, pp. 117 f., who speaks of the 'pedagogic usefulness of the cult'.

10. Altizer, *op. cit.*, p. 137.

11. Edwin Cox, *Sixth Form Religion*, London 1967, p. 97.

12. For a full discussion of this idea see I. A. Muirhead, *Education in the New Testament*, New York 1965, ch. 3.

13. Tertullian, *To His Wife*, II, 6, *Ancient Christian Writers*, vol. XIII.

14. Augustine, *Confessions*, IX, 9.

3 Children and the Bible

The present position of the Bible in the Christian churches has been well put in a single sentence: 'We thought we were agreed upon the Bible until we opened it.' This uncertainty about what the Bible is and what it is for does not make guidance about its use with children any easier. There are those who wish to give it up altogether, but they have no suggestions about what to put in its place which would preserve, as the Bible seems to do, a distinctive element in Christian nurture. There are those who would apparently dispense with God, yet wish to retain Jesus as the paradigm of true man, and yet the Bible and the Bible alone preserves the witness to him. In the midst of this confusion, the simplest preliminary to investigating what the use of the Bible with children in church might involve is to consider three possible and differing attitudes to it.

The Bible and revelation

Christians have always traced a relation between the Bible and revelation. Many of them still believe that God speaks to men out of the Bible. But what does this word 'revelation' mean? Rather than consider the question in abstract terms, this time let us look at two fairly long illustrations.

The first comes from a collection of addresses given by the famous Swiss theologian Karl Barth, when he was pastor of a small country village. To his wonderment, he discovered that quite apart from the trappings of modern scholarship with which so many of his contemporaries were concerned and in which they were totally immersed, the Bible still had a powerful message of its own and compelled its reader into a strange new world. His remarks show something of this wonderment:

We must trust ourselves to reach eagerly for an answer which is really much too large for us, for which we really are not yet ready, and of which we do not seem worthy, since it is a fruit which our own longing, striving and inner labour have not planted. What this fruit, this answer is, is suggested by the title of my address; within the Bible there is a strange new world, the world of God. This answer is the same as that which came to the first martyr, Stephen: Behold, I see the heavens opened and the Son of man standing at the right hand of God. Neither by the earnestness of our belief nor by the depth and richness of our experience have we deserved the right to this answer. What I shall have to say about it will only be a small and unsatisfying part of it. We must openly confess that we are reaching far beyond ourselves. But that is just the point: if we wish to come to grips with the contents of the Bible, we must dare to reach far beyond ourselves. The Book admits of nothing less. For, besides giving to every one of us what he rightly deserves – to one, much, to another, something, to a third, nothing – it leaves us no rest whatsoever, if we are in earnest, once with our shortsighted eyes and awkward fingers we have found the answer in it that *we* deserve. Such an answer is something but, as we soon realize, not everything. It may satisfy us for a few years, but we simply cannot be content with it for ever. Ere long the Bible says to us, in a manner candid and friendly enough, with regard to the 'versions' we make of it: 'These may be you, but they are not I! They may perhaps suit you, meeting the demands of your thought and temperament, of your era and your "circle", of your religious or philosophical theories. You wanted to be mirrored in me, and now you have really found in me your own reflection. But now I bid you come seek *me*, as well. Seek what is here.' It is the Bible itself, it is the straight inexorable logic of its onmarch which drives us out beyond ourselves and invites us, without regard to our worthiness or unworthiness, to reach for the last highest answer, in which all is said that can be said, although we can hardly understand and only stammeringly express it. And that answer is: A new world, the world of God. There is a spirit in the Bible that allows us to stop a while and play among secondary things as is our wont – but presently it begins to press us on; and however we may object that we are only weak, imperfect, and most average folk, it presses us on to the primary fact, whether we will or no. There is a river in the Bible that carries us away, once we have entrusted our destiny to it – away from ourselves to the sea. The Holy Scriptures will interpret themselves in spite of all our human limitations. We need only dare to follow this drive, this spirit, this river, to grow out beyond ourselves towards the highest answer. This daring is *faith*; and we read the Bible rightly, not when we do so with false modesty, restraint and attempted sobriety, for these are passive qualities, but when we read it in faith. And the invitation to dare and to reach toward the highest, even though we do not deserve it, is the expression of *grace* in the Bible: the Bible unfolds to us as we are met, guided, drawn on and made to grow by the grace of God.[1]

The second illustration is of a very different kind. It comes, not from a theologian, but from a novelist, D. H. Lawrence. The adolescent Ursula Brangwen is reflecting on a verse from Scripture which she had heard in church ('in church the Voice sounded . . .'):

Again she heard the Voice: 'It is easier for a camel to go through the eye of a needle than for a rich man to enter into heaven,' but it was explained that the needle's eye was a little gate for foot passengers through which the great humped camel with his load could not possibly squeeze himself; or perhaps at a great risk if he were a little camel, he might get through. For one could not absolutely exclude the rich man from heaven, said the Sunday School Teacher. It pleased him also to know that in the East one must use hyperbole or else remain unheard because the Eastern man must see a thing swelling to fill all heaven or dwindle to a mere nothing before he is suitably impressed. She immediately sympathized with this Eastern mind. Yet the words continued to have a meaning that was untouched either by the knowledge of gateways or hyperbole. The historical, local or psychological interest in the words was another thing. There remained unalterable the inexplicable value of the saying. What was this relation between a needle's eye, a rich man and heaven? What sort of needle's eye, what sort of rich man, what sort of heaven? Who knows? It means the Absolute World and can never be more than half interpreted in terms of the relative world. But must one apply the speech literally? Was her father a rich man? Couldn't he get to heaven? Or was he only a half rich man? Or was he merely a poor man? At any rate, unless he gave everything away to the poor he would find it harder to get to heaven. The needle's eye would be too tight for him. She almost wished he were penniless poor. If one were coming to the base of it, any man was rich who was not as poor as the poorest. She had her qualms when in imagination she saw her father giving away their hens and the two cows and the capital at the bank to the labourers of the district, so that by this Brangwens should be as poor as the Wherrys, and she did not want it. She was impatient. 'Very well,' she thought, 'we shall forgo that heaven, that's all – at any rate the needle's eye sort.' And she dismissed the problem. She was not going to be as poor as the Wherrys, not for all the sayings on earth. The miserable squalid Wherrys.[2]

In the contrast of these two passages, positive in the first and negative in the second in their response to the Bible, we see the point of another remark of Karl Barth's, that 'to be understood in their own sense the biblical texts call for the "No" of unbelief or the "Yes" of faith'.[3] Together, they suggest that more is involved than rational understanding and reflection on what the text says. It can bear a disclosure message, and that message requires a response. 'The Spirit shines upon the Word, And brings the truth to light.' In his *Confessions*, Augustine has perhaps the best known of all accounts of the power of the Bible:

So was I speaking, and weeping in the most bitter contrition of my heart, when, lo! I heard from a neighbouring house a voice, as of boy or girl, I know not, chanting and oft repeating, 'Take up and read; Take up and read.' Instantly, my countenance altered, I began to think most intently, whether children were wont in any kind of play to sing such words; nor could I remember ever to have heard the like. So checking the torrent of my tears, I arose; interpreting it to be no other than a command from God, to open the book, and read the first chapter I should find. For I had heard of Antony, that coming in during the reading of the Gospel, he received the admonition, as if what was being read was spoken to him: Go, sell all that thou hast, and give to the poor, and thou shalt have treasure in heaven, and come and follow me. And by such oracle he was forthwith converted unto Thee. Eagerly then I returned to the place where Alypius was sitting; for there had I laid the volume of the Apostle, when I arose thence. I seized, opened, and in silence read that section, on which my eyes first fell: Not in rioting and drunkenness, not in chambering and wantonness, not in strife and envying; but put ye on the Lord Jesus Christ, and make not provision for the flesh, in concupiscence. No further would I read; nor needed I; for instantly at the end of this sentence, by a light as it were of serenity infused into my heart, all the darkness of doubt vanished away.[4]

Similar experiences still happen today, and there is a tradition which attaches considerable importance to them. The Bible reader or teacher cannot command such an experience, although they may try in various ways to prepare for it. All, however, they can do is that:

> They must be certain (and must communicate this certainty to others) that the eye-witnesses, while expressing themselves in the language of their own time, are still able to speak to us directly when we are ready to confront their word with this faith in the Holy Spirit who is able to dispense with intermediaries.[5]

The Bible as a unity

The element of revelation understood in the terms which have just been outlined has been considerably reduced in the understanding of the Bible as presented by modern scholars. There, the Bible is seen not as a vehicle for moments of revelation but as a whole book with a unifying theme binding together even the most seemingly unrelated parts. If the first approach, roughly speaking, looked to the words to be filled with immediate meaning and power, the second, speaking equally roughly, looks to the events to have this power. The contents of the Bible are understood to be the unfolding of God's plan of salvation. The purpose of studying the Bible is thus for the reader to recognize himself and his situation in the church and his setting in history as the result of God's mighty acts summed up in the life, death and resurrection of Jesus Christ. It is for him that Abraham was called and Jesus suffered, the good news taken to the whole world and the church founded.

From this standpoint, a survey of the Bible has been

43

written under the title *The Book of the Acts of God*,[6] and it has firmly been maintained:

> Biblical theology is *the confessional recital of the redemptive acts of God* in a particular history, because history is the chief medium of revelation. The term 'history' in this connection is used in a broad sense to include not only events of seeming impersonal significance, but also the lives of individuals who compose it. The experience, the acts and the words of individuals are media of revelation, but individual personality and experience are not the centre of attention in and by themselves alone. They are the mediate means whereby God accomplishes his historical purposes, and the latter are more inclusive and comprehensive than the words, works and inner life of any one personality. The teachings of Jesus, for example, are for the Christian the revelation of the Word of God. Yet they do not form the centre of Christian theology in the sense that the expression 'God's act in Christ' presents it, nor in the sense that it is stated in the classic creeds of the Church.[7]

An approach of this kind certainly seems required by some of the contents of the Bible. A conviction of the ongoing action of God is to be seen through the Old Testament, and the words 'The promise is to you and your children', which close Peter's sermon at Pentecost, like other elements of Luke's writing, certainly require some such understanding of the book to be given to children.

Sometimes this approach is confined to the Bible, but an understanding of this kind need not separate biblical history too drastically from church history and tradition, confirming Augustine's view of a suitable curriculum for catechumens:

> The narration is complete when the beginner is first instructed from the text. In the beginning God created heaven and earth, down to the present period of church history.[8]

More, of course, is meant here than that the Bible should be regarded as a mere history book, if there is any such thing as 'mere history' in the sense of events reported without any sort of interpretation. The readers or hearers are within the particular terms of reference of this history and at the same time are involved in the community to which the acts relate. These acts are repeated ritually as in the Lord's Supper, and their effects are felt in the everyday experience of believers.

The Bible and religious experience

For some, the second approach, just mentioned, is still too simplified and too narrow. Increased understanding of the diversity of religious experience throughout the world and increased contact with those of other beliefs has led to a reluctance to put too much stress on the particularity, uniqueness or exclusiveness of Christianity. The Bible then becomes one book that often verifies experiences which those who study it may have themselves, and brings a new depth and richness into such experience. Other books can presumably do the same, and one value of this approach may be to keep reminding children that there is a sense in which the Bible is a book like other books, so that they may also grasp wherein it differs. This approach is also valuable in that it presses home the fact that the men and women of the Bible do not live in a special world of their own but are, in their essential characteristics and their ultimate problems, very like people today.

It was against this kind of view of the Bible that Karl Barth protested, as making it too much in the image of man; 'It is not the right human thoughts about God which form the content of the Bible, but the right divine thoughts about men.'[9] Thus there are many who would find it theologically insufficient in that it seems to substitute discovery for revelation. Nevertheless, the way in which it has returned with considerable force, despite the attacks made on it, seems to indicate that it represents a continuing insight which is not wholly to be ignored.

A provisional summary

These three approaches do not exhaust all the possible ways of looking at the Bible. There is also, for example, the approach which attaches importance to the close study of the most important concepts of biblical thought and their penetration in some depth. What we have seen may, however, serve to illustrate the important point that to accept the Bible as a 'given' for the purpose of Christian nurture does not at once define what use should be made of it. And at the same time it may help to define possible goals.

The three approaches need not be regarded as alternatives, for despite their apparent mutual exclusiveness each may have something of value to say. Those who would introduce children to the Bible need to be aware of this, and must ask of any method how far it is conducive to the end at which they are aiming. It could be argued from what we have seen that the purpose of using the Bible in the Christian church is to make the children of the church aware of the acts of God which created the church and made them members in it; to convince them that the God who acted in past history acts still in the present, and not only among Christians. Moreover, his ways and will can still be known, and so the Bible is in a particular way related to revelation.

The authority of the Bible

Another obvious preliminary difficulty is the nature of the Bible's authority in relation to its use with children. Does authority in this context mean that 'the Bible says' is the last word which finishes all questioning and discussion? Fundamentalism has, of course, given such authority to every jot and every tittle and, in reaction, liberalism has gone to the opposite extreme and seemed to deny the Bible any intrinsic authority in its own right. In between, church teaching has not been very clear, particularly as the divisions between confessions have either become less rigid or have been by-passed. As John McIntyre has remarked:

> It is very doubtful whether any one of us can now read scripture except through the medium of the numerous interpretative symbols which the Church has constructed to ensure our right understanding of scripture. The function of the confessions formulated by the Reformers has not always been fully appreciated in this connection. The Confessions have been, of course, correctly regarded as short summaries of the faith to be used as a basis for instructing the young and confuting heretics or unbelievers. But they also had initially a further purpose, namely that of providing the interpretative structure, for the right understanding of scripture. It is here that our present lack of confessional clarity is proving to be most harmful, in that it deprives our contemporaries, and particularly those who have to teach the young, of the adequate means of catechetical interpretation of scripture.[10]

Perhaps the place to begin a new understanding of the authority of the Bible would be to examine the nature of the authority of Jesus himself. In the Gospel picture his authority is acknowledged when it is accepted as true and acted upon; it is an authority which only proves its power in the lives of those who are prepared to learn from him and respond to his summons. It is, as it were, an authority of demonstration and response.

Such a pattern is not limited to the New Testament, but is also to be found through the Old. It forms the core of the idea of the covenant, which underlies so much of Old Testament history. God has acted for his people in delivering them from captivity; as a response, therefore, they are to follow him in doing what he commands. This pattern can be seen even in apparently the most authoritarian legal passages of Exodus and Leviticus, where so often a command is prefaced by a statement of faith or followed by an appeal to experience of what God has done. Any other kind of authority seems uncharacteristic of the Bible, nor does Jesus' 'What do you think?' suggest that the use of the Bible with children is to be governed by the principle 'Theirs not to reason why'.

Some priority will have to be allotted between these different considerations. Nevertheless, whatever the final decision and however it may influence content and method, two other considerations must be taken into account; first, the nature of the Bible itself, and second, the nature and context of the children to whom the Bible is to be introduced.

The nature of the Bible

The Bible meets children today as a book almost about another world, hardly in any respect resembling their own. This situation implies the need for some teaching about the setting of the Bible to be included in any approach to it:

> If God has condescended to address men in the full particularity of their peculiar historical and cultural environments, then we have got to immerse ourselves fully and sympathetically in those environments, with their alien customs and values, ways of thinking, and patterns of imagery, before we can understand his demand or their response.[11]

It is not, however, impossible, as some would suggest, to bridge the gulf and to introduce the children to other centuries and other conditions in lands different from their own. This is a task which children at school show themselves perfectly capable of doing and enjoying, and some of the imaginative approaches used in history and geography will already provide background to the Bible as well as suggesting how the task can be done, even in the church situation. Indeed, this may be the best kind of teaching with certain ages, and will help their understanding later on. After all, this is their history in the special sense which we considered above, and what they do in church has roots which go down deep into it.

Perhaps the gulf between the *then* and the *now* has been created by an approach that confined God to the period from Genesis to Revelation and then took up the story in individual religious experience, rather than by any difficulty which children have in learning about situations other than their own and comparing them meaningfully with their own. There are, of course, more sophisticated examples of this kind of difficulty. One of the great leading ideas which link the Testaments is the whole concept of kingship. The children, however, live in a time of disappearing kings or democratic kings. But here again the difficulty is more apparent than real. Children's stories have kings like the kings to be found in the Bible, and so does history, and the background necessary to grasp the biblical concept has been prepared for in other ways. So it can naturally be worked up and understood in its own terms, and then contrasted with present experience. In this whole field, what is to be avoided is giving the impression that Palestine is a kind of Never-Never land, and that the people of the Bible are unlike the people of any age or culture.

Another way in which the Bible is not like other books is that it is in itself a collection of books coming from different periods of time and including material from different periods within the same book. Again, this is regarded as if it were an impossible stumbling block for children, but the ingredients for a solution can be found from other subjects. Children who study English literature do it in two ways and at two levels. There is literature which makes an instant appeal, no matter when it is written and even when it is read. There is other literature which needs its context to be explained if full understanding is to be achieved.

Two examples of this in the New Testament would be chapters 8 and 13 of I Corinthians. I Corinthians 13 is a hymn to love, which, like a complete poem, could be studied in itself and has an immediate attraction; I Corinthians 8, on the other hand, with its discussion of food regulations, is impossible to understand without some knowledge of how meat and pagan temples were connected in the Corinth of the first century.

Perhaps not enough attention has been paid in dealing with the Bible to the context of the writing as an aid to understanding, even when that context can only be established in conjectural ways. Unless this is done, the impression given is of the Bible as a book of great generalities, unrelated to particular situations. Once that happens, any cross-reference from a situation *then* to a situation *now* becomes much more difficult to make. One of the great failures in the teaching of the Bible to children has been to believe that dates and authors somehow detract from the spirituality of the message. But is this really so? Or do the simple, positive results of criticism not open up new understanding of how the book came to be? This approach can be much more helpful to reading and understanding the Bible than the belief that, like the Ten Commandments in the Exodus account, it came down whole and entire from heaven. The Bible is then more easily understood as the witness of a believing community to the things that happen to them from Abraham to Christ, and the children themselves, living in such a believing community, will surely find it easier to comprehend.

A greater difficulty still, not unconnected with what has already been said, is the variety of literary forms which the Bible contains, and especially its admixture of prose and poetry, myth, legend and history, and all within a theological framework which even the most daring criticism is unable in most cases to prise away. There has often been in the past a hidden assumption that the Bible should be taken literally, especially by children, even when the authors themselves did not intend that this should be so. The nature of Bible truth was understood to be as 'it really happened'. This has made the approach of children to the Bible more wooden than their approach to any other literature. Their imagination has never been stimulated by questioning or by making them compare literary forms known to themselves with their biblical parallels. If this were done, it could only broaden and deepen their understanding of what the Bible has to say, by some understanding of the different ways it goes about saying it.

A study of *Teenage Religion* gives two views of children on the Bible. The first is correctly orthodox:

> I believe that whoever wrote the Bible was guided by God to write the truth just as it happened.

The other is 'confident unbelief':

> The Bible is just a collection of tales and songs and poetry made up by some people to explain the world in my opinion.[12]

Fear of the second has produced a use of the Bible which results in the ambiguity of the first. It also made some young people find no truth in the biblical material at the older stage because it was taught as containing only one kind of truth which later they could no longer accept – and which was possibly not even the truth which the writer intended to convey.

There is much to be said for the recent contention that 'too much Biblical material is used too soon and too frequently.'[13] The children were being asked to sit down and eat before the meal was properly cooked, or they were provided with the necessary cutlery to eat it. If this situation is to be avoided and proper attention given to the complex

51

biblical factors detailed above, there will be need for a selection and graded use of the Bible material, beginning with stories of the people in both Testaments, and especially stories of Jesus, which relate to the children's own experience in their families and in the church family; working on from this the teaching and experience needs to be related more to the setting of the Bible events than to events themselves, although these will always be in view: then a survey of the main events, Exodus, monarchy, prophecy, exile; the Baptist, Jesus, the preaching of the Gospel, to give the thread of the story of salvation: next, enquiry into the nature of the Bible as a book and how it came to be; last, building up what the Bible teaches about God, about Jesus, about the Holy Spirit, about man.

Such a scheme in broad outline might be a guide to the approach to be followed. So far it looks like an academic study, but, in the end, and even on the way to the end, the children should be receiving

a creative communication in which the dead is made alive, the old new, and the learner provided with a quality of insight which makes him wise.[14]

This means wise, not in the sense that he possesses more biblical information, but that he is given new ways of looking at his own world and life here and now. An example of what this implies was shown when a class of teenage boys, well used to the ideology of a society where equal pay for equal work was the rule, discovered that Jesus' parable of the labourers in the vineyard was apparently operating on a quite different scale of values altogether.

Two modern theologians have made suggestions which are relevant to the approach which is being suggested here. Paul van Buren writes:

It is nothing short of amazing that preachers still use, in whatever way, biblical texts, still make reference to biblical passages. What sense can this make to those who do not even know the stories of the Bible? In order that the particular story or the particular form of the whole Christian story which is being told at any one time may be heard with even a fraction of the fullness which the preacher intends, it is necessary that the listeners know the whole range of biblical stories. If they do not learn these stories in Sunday School or Bible class, where shall they learn them? What is Easter without the story of Mary and the Gardener and also the story of the Exodus? What is Christmas without the Nativity stories of both Matthew and Luke? What is Christian love without the stories of the Good Samaritan and Lazarus and the rich man? Stories can be taught and learned. That is the task of Christian education.

Christian education involves the teaching of the stories of Christian faith as stories. If refugees spend most of their time telling the story of their lives, it is because telling stories does something which listing statistics does not. A good story, which as a story serves a certain purpose, may no longer serve that purpose if transposed into a 'record of facts', whatever that may be. If believers are to benefit by hearing the Christian story, it might be well for them to be shown that stories have important functions to perform. Deprive man of his stories, make him unable to tell and hear stories, and you make him by that much a poorer creature. . . .

He who serves in the work of Christian education serves faith, therefore, by teaching the role which story-telling plays in human life, in the hopes of winning a frame of mind that will appreciate stories, not as 'facts', not as 'critical history', but as stories, as one of men's important ways of winning understanding and being understood.[15]

There are certainly points in Van Buren's general approach at which he seems to go not nearly far enough in what he feels able to say about the truth of Christianity. But here what he says is surely to be accepted as a minimum. This is the frame of mind that one would wish to introduce to children for their encounter with the Bible.

Paul Tillich takes the argument a stage further:

The great art of the religious educator is to transform the primitive literalism with regard to the symbols into a conceptual interpretation without changing the power of the symbols.[16]

Many despair of such a possibility. They either refuse to help the pupil in the necessary transformation or they refuse to give him the traditional symbols before he is able to interpret them conceptually. Both ways are wrong.[17]

The Bible should be used, then, not merely to help children 'know the Bible', but that they grow progressively in their thinking about the Christian faith and its application to everyday life.

Perhaps as a footnote to what has just been said may be added a plea that, when children actually come to read the Bible for themselves, the portions will be of such length and character and so within the range of their vocabulary and interest that they will have a sense of achievement rather than frustration. Many adults today will not read the Bible because they were never introduced to it in any way that made sense to them. An impression was made of long words, long passages, in small print, producing an almost physical aversion to later encounters. The technical vocabulary need not be too difficult for children, who can master complex vocabularies in other fields, provided that the words are explained and not regarded as self-communicating. Modern translations have their own part to play in this; in particular, Alan Dale's *New World*[18] shows remarkably well how the New Testament can go into children's language and still lose nothing of its effect and power.

Children and their development

So far the Bible has been the centre of consideration, although the children's reactions and possibilities have been included, but the general thrust of the argument needs correction, as it may have left the impression that to make the Bible easier to read and understand, and in an intellectual way, is all that is required, and that this is the prime necessity for its communication. But:

54

This necessity cannot be met from the Gospel side only, as though it were merely a matter of translating the word into such simple speech that it would be intelligible to any reasonable human being at any stage of development. By all means let us distribute our Moffatt's translations and our New Testaments in Basic English, but the fundamental problem of our time is not merely that of re-translating the Christian gospel, it is to express it in our own psychological situation. 'No man can come to me except the Father draw him.' The text teaches that there are more factors present in the acceptance of Christian truth than merely its presentation. There is also something at work within the human soul moving it to the angle from which it can see the truth.[19]

The plain effect of this is to suggest that there are times in the life of children when one kind of material will be more useful than another because it is related to an interest already there, or answers a question which is already being asked, or meets a need already felt. Child psychologists have claimed to be able to furnish such information, and this might imply that grading and selection must take this factor also into account. Here is still an area of controversy between psychologists who wish to direct, and theologians who refuse to be directed. Certainly, the confusion in this area in the past has produced some most unsuitable selections of parts of the Bible for teaching purposes, for example that of John 20 as a lesson for children under the rubric 'A Picnic on the Shore'. Nine-year-olds have been made to study the story of Elisha and the bears (II Kings 2.23 ff.), presumably for the reason that children of this age would be interested in animals! Further, the attempt to enlist children's proclivity towards hero worship has had some curious results, especially in the presentation of Jesus. Those who really understand the kind of hero who does appeal to the modern child have tended to colour the presentation so that often Jesus ceases to be the Jesus of the Gospel witness. A similar difficulty is created by our heroes-of-long-ago approach to some of the figures of the Old Testament and to the disciples in the New, who, in the educative process, lose the very qualities which earn them their place in the biblical record.

There is, however, perhaps a deeper difficulty still. The Bible does not only meet need. At the same time it creates new needs. (Jesus' conversation at the well with the woman of Samaria (John 4) is a good illustration of how this process might work.) It does not only help men to meet their difficulties, but has faced them with new difficulties over the course of history. Race and colour, for example, have become problems for many Christian men and women who as children happily absorbed the kindness of the Samaritan but must now ask themselves about the coloured man next door, 'Is he my neighbour?' There is just a suggestion in some attempts to relate psychology and the Bible, that the Bible will always be a panacea and never a two-edged sword. Such an approach, consistently followed, would justify Freud's criticism of religion and place the Bible among the childlike things which a man could well do without. Yet, when this has been said, it may nevertheless be the typical blast of the theological trumpet to scare a foe who is really an ally all the time. No one can lightly set about the task of the Christian upbringing of children without taking into account the new knowledge of children, how they learn, what interests and helps them, what are the real questions with which they are concerned.

Paul Tillich makes the point developed above in another way:

> Religious induction faces two main difficulties. One is the fact that it has to give answers to questions that have never been asked by the child. Therefore every religious educator must try to find the existentially important questions which are alive in the minds and hearts of the pupils.[20]

One of the great and helpful contributions of Harold

Loukes' study *Teenage Religion* was that by going directly to young people themselves and allowing them opportunity to express their thoughts, he showed what concerned and troubled them at this stage and offered guidance on appropriate biblical material (and the use of it) which would make it more possible for them to hear the word of God.

Ronald Goldman has tried to do the same for a younger age group by suggesting that the approach should be through 'life-themes' which follow through experience known to the children and include within them religious elements as part of the whole project. The benefit of the method is in a sense to bring the Bible in manageable portions within the area of the children's already aroused interest and concern.[21] Both of these contributions, whatever one may think of their particular working out in practical suggestions, cannot be neglected in any consideration of how the Bible is to be commended to children in the church situation. There need be no fear that attention in this area may result in such attenuated syllabuses that all the preliminary considerations with which this chapter began will be frustrated. On the contrary, the two go very much together. One writer, at least, obviously does not expect children to do less, but to do more along the lines which will be most effective:

The child will absorb only those elements that correspond to his mental interest; on the other hand, it is of advantage to have his mind stretched along the lines of his natural growth. . . . They are more likely to be given too little than too much information. They can stand up to hard work of the right sort. They are capable of absorbing a good deal of objective information about religious matters. It needs to be factual, with the aim of teaching the children the contents of the Bible, the history of its formation, what the church believes by way of doctrine, what the various services of the church mean. All this needs to be graded to what the child can understand. Provided he can link it up to his own situation, he can take any amount of information.[22]

Conclusion

It is important not to close this chapter without drawing attention to certain considerations which are often forgotten when the place of the Bible in nurture is being discussed. The first is the context where the Bible is introduced (apart from its setting in services of worship). The point has been made that:

> Every exchange between husband and wife, parent and child, teacher and pupil, person and person, has more meaning than the thing talked about. What happens between men is of primary importance and provides an enabling or disabling context for the purpose of whatever exchange takes place between them.[23]

This consideration, although it has been kept to the end, is obviously as important as all that has gone before. A context of love seems almost a necessity for understanding a book which proclaims itself as a message from a God of love. There is a happy illustration in John Chrysostom of what is implied here. He speaks about a father patiently telling his child a story from the Bible. Then the mother tells him the story again. The child is prompted by the parents to tell it over to them, and is interested in their interest. Father and son then go to church and the same story is read and the child beams with pride because he has heard it before. All very simple, all very domesticated, but all very important. And, Chrysostom adds, 'hereafter the episode is fixed in his memory'. This experience has been true for many, that the importance of the Bible and its value were first received unconsciously from the context and not consciously from the content, although one became the introduction to the other.

A second point is rather more debatable. The Bible can be seen as well as heard. The answer sometimes given by the Catholics to the Reformers who proclaimed that they had taken the Bible out of the hands of the people, was to claim that on the contrary they had opened it up to them in ways which they could understand through sacrament, symbol, picture and stained glass. The whole matter of the use of pictures in teaching the Bible seems neither to be answered by the Heidelberg Catechism's 'No' nor by an equally enthusiastic 'Yes' which assumes that because visual aids have helped elsewhere, they will help here. It should, however, be noted that factual pictures of the lands of the Bible and biblical archaeology promote understanding as well as verbal explanation, and that some of the great paintings on biblical themes are in their own way like commentaries on the text of the Bible and do awaken insights in unexpected ways.

Thirdly, a warning should be issued against only using the Bible with a view to bringing out some kind of moral application. The relation of the Bible to conduct will be discussed later in this book; meanwhile, it is sufficient to say that attention to the message of the Bible has been frustrated in children because of the impression constantly given that some general word of application at the end was the really worthwhile thing, like the classic, 'This shows, children, that we should all be like king Solomon'!

It would be no less valuable for the children of this generation to have as part of their Christian nurture such an introduction to the Bible as will convince them of its worth as the means for understanding their life both in the church and world, showing that it is able to afford fresh and compelling insights, bringing together past and present in moments of illumination. Here is a resource for nurture which has its best effect when it is seen as something never grown beyond or grown out of, because it is always relevant. If the methods suggested above can take away the stumbling blocks which have tended to keep the young back from it, and if adults support this by an example of use which shows its worth for them, the rest is work for the Holy Spirit to do. But the Spirit cannot bring the truth to light where the book is never opened and never read.

NOTES

1. Karl Barth, *The Word of God and the Word of Man*, New York 1957, pp. 33 f.

2. D. H. Lawrence, *The Rainbow*, Penguin edition, p. 233.

3. Karl Barth, *Evangelical Theology*, London 1963, p. 165.

4. Augustine, *Confessions*, Book VIII, ch. 12, quoted from the translation by Rex Warner, Mentor Omega books, New York 1963.

5. Oscar Cullmann, *The Early Church*, London 1956, pp 97 f.

6. G. E. Wright and R. H. Fuller, *The Book of the Acts of God*, London 1961.

7. G. E. Wright, *God Who Acts*, London 1952, p. 13.

8. Augustine, *First Catechetical Instruction*, III, 5, *Ancient Christian Writers*, vol. II, p. 18.

9. Karl Barth, *The Word of God and the Word of Man*, p. 43.

10. John McIntyre, *The Shape of Christology*, pp. 20 f.

11. D. E. Nineham, *The Church's Use of the Bible Past and Present*, London 1963, p. 161.

12. Harold Loukes, *Teenage Religion*, London 1961, p. 41.

13. Ronald Goldman, *Readiness for Religion: A Basis for Developmental Religious Education*, London 1965, p. 7

14. J. Stanley Glen, *The Recovery of the Teaching Ministry*, p. 62.

15. Paul van Buren, *Theological Explorations*, London 1968, pp. 70 f.

16. Paul Tillich, *Theology of Culture*, New York 1959, p. 115.

17. *Ibid.*, p. 156.

18. Published by Oxford University Press, one volume edition 1968.

19. Erastus Evans, 'Phases of Psychic Life', in *Christian Essays in Psychiatry*, ed. Philip Mairet, London 1956.

20. Paul Tillich, *Theology of Culture*, p. 154.

21. See Ronald Goldman, *Readiness for Religion*, pp. 111–18, for examples of such life-themes.

22. R. S. Lee, *Your Growing Child and Religion*, Penguin Books 1965, p. 170.

23. Reuel Howe, *The Miracle of Dialogue*, New York 1963, p. 38.

4 Children at Prayer

A case was made in Chapter 2 for including 'the means of grace' in the 'given' for the nurture of Christian children. Now we must look more closely at this and what it means for the children in the two most obvious areas: public worship – which will include the sacrament of Baptism and the Lord's Supper – and private prayer, which will be considered along with family worship.

The very names of these exercises have a slightly dated sound in this theological space age, and both have been under fire from critics who themselves are within the Christian faith. Worship as it happens in most churches on most Sundays has been criticized as an attempt to make man look for God and the encounter with him where it will not happen, for God is where the action is, and the action is not in church. Private prayer as conventionally understood and practised is condemned as too juvenile an approach to God for men come of age, like running to father instead of standing up for oneself.

These would be serious criticisms indeed if one did not feel all the time that in the eyes of the critics worship and action are regarded as incompatible and unable to exist side by side without the one spoiling the other, in particular, worship turning men's eyes away from the world where God is to be served. It may, however, be that what is really being attacked is not the use but the abuse of worship, and this would be in line with the Old Testament prophets and with Jesus' own attitude to the temple. Certainly, no

Christian parent can approve of a nurture which does not have life in this world in view, and no parent nowadays would wish his children shielded from the reality of life, even if the child would allow it. After all, the Christian devotional symbol is a cross, the gas chamber or electric chair or firing squad of the first century, for those who offended against the régime. The worldly factual reality is there even when the cross is lovingly carved in wood as the original never would be, or made in precious metal or encrusted with jewels. But these decorated crosses may be in themselves parables of what the critics mean, that the real world can be lost sight of in worship. Equally, however, in action, the reason for action can be lost and it can become meaningless activity. Nevertheless, in considering what participation in any form of worship will mean for children, these positive contributions of the critics must be kept in mind.

The nature of worship

What, then, are the conventions, if this is the right word, on which these assemblies of the faithful, usually associated with Sundays, operate? Essentially, worship is the acknowledgment of worth. So Christians come together to express the value that they put upon God. Expressed in this way, it would appear the most human and subjective of enterprises – a God with a hundred names, with as vague a scale of values attached to him as there are people present. But this is to look at the whole affair the wrong way round. As we argued before, it is God who is to be given chief place. It is God who has shown his worth, and every service of worship, whether through the reading of the Bible, the preaching of the word or the celebration of the sacraments, declares what God has shown himself to be. The very meeting on Sunday, the first day of the week when

Jesus rose from the dead, is itself a way of declaring that this act of God in Jesus is the *reason* for the assembly. Christians have to come together again to share the source of the new life which they believe has come to them through Jesus Christ.

Iris Murdoch illustrates this well in her novel *The Red and the Green*:

> Today was Palm Sunday and Andrew, together with his mother and fiancée, Frances Bellman, had attended matins at the Mariners' Church in Kingstown. On emerging from the church they had found the street filled with those others who, streaming in far greater numbers out of their chapels, were now parading about, more slowly, more confidently, carrying palms in their hands. For them it seemed, and for their sins, Christ was even now entering Jerusalem, and their demeanour exhibited already a satisfaction, even a possessiveness.[1]

It is for this reason that Bishop John Robinson speaks of the Eucharist as 'the Christian action . . . the heart of all Christian action in the world',[2] and Dom Gregory Dix tells of Christians in times of persecution who would risk death rather than miss coming together for the sacrament.

When Paul hands down the tradition 'Do this in remembrance of me', he uses a word whose biblical flavour is exactly and convincingly caught in Iris Murdoch's quotation. It means re-living and re-presenting, so that as the Christian acknowledges the worth of what God has done in worship, he prepares himself to express the same worth in his life every day. For the Christian, the far off divine event has become present reality and ultimate hope, because to the group of people to which he belongs, true life is life in Christ. He is the one who is worthy. As the paraphrase of Revelation 5.6 has it:

> Worthy the Lamb that died, they cry,
>   To be exalted thus;
> Worthy the Lamb, our lips reply,
>   For he was slain for us.

Acknowledgment of what this implies is expressed by the recital of creeds in some churches; in almost all by the use of words of praise, spoken or sung, whether biblical, like the Psalms and Canticles, or non-biblical, like the anthems and hymns. It also finds expression in prayers of different kinds, all nevertheless reflecting the nature of the God to whom they are offered through Jesus Christ. (The classical divisions of Christian prayer are only meaningful in relation to what God has shown himself to be.) It finds expression, too, in the eucharistic offering of bread and wine, in the token money offered, and what all such offering implies.

> Present your bodies as a living sacrifice, holy and acceptable to God, which is your spiritual worship. Do not be conformed to this world but be transformed by the renewal of your mind, that you may prove what is the will of God, what is good and acceptable and perfect.

So wrote Paul at the beginning of Romans 12, and the whole of the chapter, with the one that follows, shows the kind of worldly holiness that this will involve. The same connection is expressed in many ways. The Roman Mass in Latin finishes with the words 'Missa est', the origin of the word 'Mass' itself. The phrase literally means, 'It's all over'. But a Roman Catholic writer comments:

> It is the spirit of the extraordinary short final part of the Roman Mass to interpret it as a kind of sending out on a mission. Thus one's daily work becomes a continuation of the Mass.[3]

A Methodist minister makes the same point rather differently:

> Worship is that sort of recognition of God's activity that allows him to penetrate and permeate the whole of the worshipper's world.[4]

What has been said above is an attempt at a description of the kind of activity which worship is. It is obviously independent of any liturgical form or any particular kind of place of meeting, and it could be independent of particular days or seasons, although the first day of the week directly remembers Jesus crucified and risen and the main days of the Christian year tellingly repeat God's action in Christ. The essential, however, is a fellowship of believing people who consider this kind of encounter with God necessary to their lives and to be found only through this coming together and living again what God has done in order to enrol them again in his service. The two facets of worship are presented in parable form in Isaiah 6. The prophet sees the temple filled with the glory of the Lord and is so overwhelmed that he can do nothing but confess his lostness; but the scene ends with the voice of this Lord asking whom he is to send and the response of the prophet, cleansed and renewed, 'Here I am! Send me.' Here is the recognition of the presence of God and the recognition of the obligation to serve him in the world which it lays upon the worshippers.

Of course, different churches will hold their services in different ways and put their emphasis on different parts, but enough has been said to show what will be involved in introducing children to this kind of worship so that they can share in it meaningfully. Again, as has already been remarked in connection with the Bible, the most desirable thing for the children is that they shall find reality in such a service – and this, in the last resort, is not something that can be commanded at will:

> The church has not the divine presence at its disposal and cannot conjure it up by an automatic process which it might use as it pleases.[5]

It is good to be clear about this at the start. The church can strive to have its children present at worship; it cannot guarantee to make them worship, and those who believe that brighter, or simpler, or shorter services will without fail achieve this do not rightly understand the nature of the enterprise in which they are engaged. This, however, does not mean that nothing from the human side can be done, or that there are no stumbling-blocks to be taken out of the way.

Children in church

It has been said that the children of the church have a right to be in church. But what children? And for how long? And what kind of share should they be expected to take in what goes on? Should special recognition be made of them as children and young people, although they belong as much as any adult Christian? These questions certainly demand an answer. So far, what has been offered is a theological justification for their presence, but there are non-theological factors on the other side. There is the actual physical discomfort that can be produced by short legs and high pews (shades of Augustine with his concern that his catechumens should be 'sitting comfortably'!). There is the mental indigestion of listening to long prayers and sermons, for the most part incomprehensible to them. Most serious of all, there is the objection put by John Robinson from the experience of his own family:

> Despite the fact that our children have been at Parish Communion almost every Sunday of their lives from the carry-cot onwards, it was becoming increasingly clear that most of it simply passed them by, because the service in church corresponded with nothing concrete in their everyday experience and relationships.[6]

Yet these things do not need to be in order to have the essentials of worship as presented above, especially when it is worship of the whole body of the faithful of whom it can be said now, as then, 'Few of you are men of wisdom, by any known standard' (I Cor. 1.26). Moreover, there are ways of making truth plain other than verbalization. There are the sacraments themselves, and symbolic actions ancient and modern, like that described by Iris Murdoch; and there are possibilities like a reminiscence of a Whitsunday scene in Holland:

> I remember a Whitsunday service in the Domchurch in Utrecht, Holland. The Reformation certainly made something 'honest and sober' out of that building, but ruined it in the process. On this Whitsunday, all the Sunday school children of the town paraded through it, surrounding the austere Calvinists and their classic pews, playing on biblical instruments – drums, tambourines and flutes. And I am sure that the congregation got more of the joy of Pentecost out of the ear-splitting music (?) those children made than out of whatever the preachers had to say that morning.[7]

Not all churches can or will use such variations in worship as make it easier for children to take an active part. After all, what is wanted is not gimmicks to amuse the children and keep them quiet, but to enable them to take as much share as they can. But there seems to be no good reason to keep them out, at least which cannot be overcome, and every good reason to have them in. It does not seem to be always true, though it is obviously so for a vocal few, that attendance at church as a child, especially with one's parents, gives a lasting distaste for public worship. Such evidence as there is (and so many factors are involved that reliable evidence is difficult to come by), would suggest that such attendance is more likely to promote a continuing love for worship than artificial segregation from it, until such time that it is decided that sufficient maturity has been reached for meaningful participation.

The answer here, as in the case of the Bible, may lie in a gradual familiarization of children with church. It is desirable that all children should come, and the best way for them to come is to come as soon as they are able, and preferably at four years of age, so that the church can be a new world to them outside the home, even before the school. The parents should bring them. The smallest might sit for only a short time, and then go out, if possible to some kind of creche with suitable activities for their age. They might return, especially when a baptism is held at the end of the service, or even during the last hymn, for the Benediction.

A good preparation for all this would be a weekday visit to the church, when they would be able to move around and see what is out of sight on Sunday, hear how loud the organ is and accustom themselves to the different rules for Sunday when the church has other people, when movement is formalized and talking out loud is not encouraged. This stage might last from age four to seven or eight.

Children between eight and eleven-plus might stay for a longer time. This part of the service might then become a kind of catechumen's service not all directed towards the children, but remembering that the children are present, in choosing the lessons, if choice is free, in introducing the lessons, if a lectionary is followed, or in choosing and introducing hymns. The prayers would include concrete situations recognizable by the children, and some parts of thanksgiving and intercession should seek to move within their experience, as well as making them familiar with the more formal and general. There might be a children's address, not the moral tale nor the parable from fable to life for which most in this group are not ready, but better related to what is seen and done at the actual service of worship. The church's education programme for these children should reinforce this with teaching about what happens in church and relating it to suitable biblical material. This would have a double effect. It would help the children to take more interest in what went on in the service, and it would provide a forum for discussion of the things which they might want to ask. This second group might on some occasions stay for the whole service, and on others be brought back in the same ways as the younger group.

At the magic age of eleven-plus, children should be encouraged to stay for the whole service. The worth of this procedure is that it does recognize how much most children like to do what adults do, especially when loving and beloved adults are prepared to do it with them. Of course, the objective is maximum participation. Real worship as personal response lies in no human hand. Eagerness to come, enjoyment when present, growing understanding of what is happening, and why, increasing outward participation, these can be worked for by parents and teachers and by the adult congregation whose own attitude at worship is most likely to be the children's model. We must keep in mind how limited the objective is:

> They can be trained to imitate the behaviour of adults at worship. They can sing hymns, say prayers, no doubt, too, they get interest out of it. All that may have its value, but it is not religion and not worship, for young children cannot understand the abstract ideas involved in worship. But none the less one of the facts of their environment is the practice of worship, private and public. It is something they cannot help noticing. It is right that children should explore this fact and be given opportunity to participate. They should be allowed to attend Divine Worship with their parents, and this should be presented as a privilege, as if it were something for grown-ups which children cannot be expected to understand, something they will come to later on. Too much should not be expected of them.[8]

The age of understanding

It has been suggested that some falling away is to be expected, temporary perhaps in the case of some, but permanent in the case of others. The most likely time for this to happen is around adolescence, if not before. It can happen even when parents are diligent and devoted and make attendance at worship an obvious priority for which all other things except 'works of necessity and mercy' are set aside, as well as in the more likely cases where to be like father, old enough *not* to go to church, is perhaps a deciding factor. Young people of this age do not want so much to do what the family does, or will only do it if they feel like doing it for its own sake. There will be other factors at work here also: the influence of friends who have no connection with church or no interest in it, or who belong to another denomination. The result can be a conflict of loyalties. The same thing can happen because of the absence of other children from the same school or neighbourhood in the church group at this age.

In so complex a situation, the degree to which the congregation is able to make the child feel known and wanted is all-important. Speaking of the reaction of her three children to a new scheme of church education, a mother remarked: 'The other two went because I wanted them to go; he wants to go himself.' This is what is desired, and so perhaps for that very reason some churches look to this period of adolescence as the time when what was received in baptism is acknowledged or confirmed. This will involve some profession or confession from the young person that he now wishes to remain of his own free will where God has placed him in the church. Whereas formerly he *was* enrolled, now he enrols himself. Such decision and confessing are sometimes associated with admission to the Lord's Supper if this is regarded as a fitting place. The benefit of such a structuring is its progression towards a more full and personal participation as a chosen sharer until the very heart of Christian worship is reached.

Here the practices of the church vary. There are two attitudes which might need re-examining. The first question to consider is whether this deciding and confessing, in whatever way churches wish to provide for it, is related to receiving communion, or whether the baptized cannot receive communion as early as baptism itself, as is the Eastern Orthodox practice. It is easy to dismiss such an approach as promoting superstition, but it can certainly also increase the sense of belonging and participation in the church in the same way as other members of the Christian family. Is it more or less magic to recite the Lord's Prayer without understanding, or to sing 'Jesus loves me' without understanding, or to receive the sacrament which says without words, 'Whatever others receive, you receive'? The fullness of the reception, like the fullness of prayer and hymn, can only develop with time and faith. Here is an area of great difficulty, with problems of church order and theology to be solved, as well as the best nurture of the children.

The second question to be considered is whether this deciding and confessing should be related even roughly to any special age, at which such a step might be looked for and the best preparation for it made. Phrases used in this connection are 'years of discretion' and 'the age of reason'. Some Catholic authorities have declared that seven is such an age. One notable authority, however, is of the opinion that the present canon law, which suggests admission to first communion at seven, is capable of being interpreted less rigidly:

> The dignity of the Sacrament is safeguarded in so far as it is to be administered to the children only when they are able to receive it with some understanding . . . it is for the confessors and parents and guardians to judge.[9]

The Evangelicals, too, in their day regarded childhood as a time for decision, although they never tied themselves to a precise age. Yet this is the sentiment of John Burton's hymn for children:

> Saviour, while my heart is tender,
> I would yield that heart to Thee;
> All my powers to Thee surrender,
> Thine and only Thine to be.

Presumably there would be adults, too, to judge the reality of any confession made. So in more than one tradition there has been a tendency to make the age early, although always there is an expectation that the children will grow either sacramentally or in their religious experience, or even in their intellectual understanding. Thus this is always a process begun, and not by any means a finished work.

At the other end of the scale, and in many churches, there is a tendency to make 'years of discretion' conform a little more nearly to the varying ages of responsibility decided upon by society and to admit at an older age. This is a curious tendency at a time when young people are maturing earlier and making other quite important decisions for themselves at a young age. Yet it may be allied with a new seriousness about religion and a new unwillingness to be committed until one is sure, especially of the true nature and extent of the commitment. The whole question is complex. The young wish to be sure, but how sure can one be? *Credo* has been translated, 'I am prepared to bet my life that this is so'. Certainly this kind of assurance is required, but not the assurance which claims to have solved all mysteries. Nor can discipleship be defined in specific terms in advance of the situation, or commitment be expressed exactly. 'I believe, help thou my unbelief' is still the model confession, and it obviously needs some maturity for the making.

The emphasis of the Anglican Prayer Book and the Scottish *First Book of Discipline* of 1560, which consider an ability to say the Creed, the Ten Commandments and the Lord's Prayer as the ground for admission to communion or

Confirmation (see 'The Order for Confirmation' and 'A Short Sum of the First Book of Discipline'), do follow what has been called 'the Agreed Syllabus of the early church', and the catechism serves to explain these three symbols. The trouble, however, at any rate in Scotland, was that intellectual grasp or even sheer ability to repeat information could be confused with genuine decision and discipleship. Equally wrong is, of course, the opposite, where sentimental profession based on feeling and lacking the backbone of information is accepted without any attempt to show either the need for some intellectual understanding or what will be involved in daily living.

What brings young people forward will always remain a mystery of the working of the Spirit. All that the churches can do is to provide an opportunity for the coming and a structure for learning something of what is involved. Augustine's advice was to try to find out what brings them, and yet to recognize behind some of the quite worldly reasons and social pressures that another Spirit is here at work. Social pressures to be involved in the church are less likely now than they were a few years ago, but they still influence some. Doctrinaire views on the right age or the wrong age are less likely to be helpful here, and even good classes for instruction are insufficient, unless there goes with them good, skilful pastoral counselling of a non-directive kind, which will enable a young man or woman brought up in the church to come to a responsible decision about remaining in it. Perhaps some of the failure in this area at the present time has come about because the decisions seem only to relate to service in church and not to the service of Christ in the world.

Family worship

We have looked first at worship in the sense of community

worship with word and sacrament at its heart, for while there are pleas for liturgical renewal, and warnings of the difficulty of observing the Lord's Day in an industrial society geared to shift-work, the thing in itself retains its meaning and stands as a necessity for Christians. More serious are the criticisms which see common worship as somehow divorced from the common life, especially when it ceases to be at the centre of the life of a small, self-contained community. The group is artificial and unknown to one another ('All these unknown people in their unusual clothes'), and this can increase the difficulty of introducing children into it.

In the early days of Christianity, for some children their own home would be the church, and for others, going to church would be like visiting neighbours and friends. Indeed, it would take place in so domestic an atmosphere that an early liturgy had to include the direction, 'Mothers, take up your children', lest the young ones would get in the way of those who were bringing up the offering. There may be a need for the restoration of some form of family worship, like the experiment with his own family which Bishop John Robinson describes:

A dissatisfaction with family prayers, with communion preparation, with grace before meals – together with the fact that I was so frequently out when the children were home – combined to make us resolve to set aside one meal in the week (at present supper on Saturday), to which we would all give a priority and which we would make a sort of family celebration. It is not a Eucharist, but a rather special meal, to which we all look forward, which includes a bottle of wine. The procedure is extremely flexible, but at the moment we normally begin (in winter) by lighting the table candles and singing the very early Christian hymn, 'Hail, gladdening Light'. Then in prayer we share freely whatever is concerning us, our doings and our relations, bringing in also those with whom we shall be meeting at the Lord's Table the next morning. At the close of this we say together an adapted verse of a eucharistic hymn:

> Come, risen Lord and deign to be our guest;
> Nay, let us be thy guests; the feast is thine;
> Thyself at thine own board make manifest,
> In this our fellowship of bread and wine.

I then cut a slice from the loaf and pour out a glass of wine, both of which we pass around, ending with a salutation, or the grace, and a joining of hands. After the meal we do some Bible study based on the Epistle or the Gospel for the next day, and end the evening by playing a family game.[10]

Such experiences in the home will help to break down the strangeness of the similar actions when they take place in the larger family, in the church. It is interesting how what Bishop Robinson says envisages such a bridging, in the content of the prayers, where 'we share freely what is concerning us, our doings and our relations, bringing in also those whom we shall be meeting at the Lord's Table next morning'. So the two families are related in a meaningful way. The child's sense of the importance of worship to his parents will increase when he finds worship not limited to special church occasions but as part of the ongoing life of the home as well.

In this way, too, some of the language gulf may be bridged. In church, even what is relevant and within grasp is sometimes not heard because it is not listened to. Prayers in the home which would reflect on the circumstances of the shared life, the joys and sorrows of neighbours, world needs as these come into the home with Christian Aid collections and flag days, or events in newspapers and television, could lead to better listening to church prayers which must inevitably express themselves for the most part in generalized terms to cover the needs of the larger group.

Perhaps there is unwillingness to begin here because family prayers conjure up a picture of the Victorian dining-room, with all present and correct. The instance of Lord Ebury in *The Lilac and the Rose*, shows what could happen:

These extempore prayers interpolated always when the subject of them was present, and kneeling with his elbows on one of the red leather chairs in a particularly defenceless position were, I am sure, a great satisfaction to his lordship, who, under the cloak of a petition to the Deity, could safely admonish his recalcitrant children.[11]

The old, however, need not be the pattern for the new. Parents who seriously begin to experiment with new ways will find both difficulty and renewal, because sharing life with their children involves sharing God and his life with them. Indeed, it might help enormously in all this if such worship in the family did have a larger counterpart in some kind of neighbourhood groups or shared-interest groups meeting for worship. These could then become introductory stages towards the larger church, where the children could go with their own family and recognize the members of their own group. To introduce stages in this way would give a new expression to the whole life of the church and bind its worship more closely to the roots of ordinary life. The result might be that public worship itself would learn to express larger group concern in its whole structuring, rather than the individual pietism into which it can so easily fall at present.

Experiments of this kind can be quite far-reaching. Here is one indication of what has already taken place:

The Protestant community of Taizé has, in its own way, fought for a new integration of life and worship through the total, lifelong commitment of the brothers; the community of Iona has done the same thing, combining social and political action with a rather elaborate worship life. But why cannot our parishes and conferences do the same thing? Why should we not bring into our service of worship the products of our hands – the factory-made articles, the books that have been written and the newspapers that have been distributed? Why should not, in each service, a layman speak briefly about the area of life in which he is engaged? Should not the prayer of intercession always begin with some short, well-prepared introduction into the problem that the congregation wants to lift up to God?

76

One of the most impressive services of worship I have ever seen was in a Western European country with many political parties, in which a group of congregations came together during the election campaign to sing and pray, and to have their own members, engaged in different parties, simply and without propagandist motives explain why they voted for one party and not for another. Is that not worship? The reintegration of all life into our worship will probably be as painful a process as we have gone through while losing it all, but is it not worth it?[12]

This kind of approach could be adapted to take account of children's needs, too, thus achieving the variety and flexibility which so many plead for, and plead for on the children's behalf. Worship, too, would become associated with other places than the church, other times than Sunday, other leaders than the clergy. In addition, children would continue to worship in Sunday schools and Bible classes and youth groups; here there could be increasing participation by the children themselves in conducting such services and therefore being prepared to take a share in the conducting of the larger services as well.

Private prayer

We must now consider private prayer – what it is, what it should be and whether children can be introduced to this form of devotion which has been so characteristic of the Christian faith. Christians see themselves as able to bring their concerns to God, not only in the fellowship of the church but individually.

The Old Testament remarks how 'The Lord used to speak to Moses as a man speaks to his friend' (Ex. 33.11), and this basic characteristic is confirmed by what the Gospels tell of the prayers and the prayer-life of Jesus. There is here a rhythm of withdrawal from the world to be with God, and in his strength to go back to the world. It is fashionable to draw attention to the crude anthropomorphism of this conception, and yet the alternatives suggested even by the critical scarcely seem to measure up to what Jesus Christ has revealed of his Father and the loving relationship with God which is like that of a man with his friend, and belongs within the same area of personal relations. It is because one knows what commitment to others means that one can pray to God as one who is himself committed to others: 'Forgive us our debts as we forgive our debtors.'

The reality of private prayer for children will begin when they are able to see the difference between praying and saying prayers. Joyce Kenwrick records an experience related to her, which is perhaps important here:

> Never at any time did the conviction leave me that God existed, but again and again he seemed irrelevant. When I was over forty years old, in a moment of great stress, there came the utter conviction that the spiritual life was a reality. It came through seeing another person, not 'saying prayers' but praying, and completely unaware that I was there. I am quite unable to explain why that experience should have had the force of a hard physical blow, and a shock of surprise that is as vivid now as it was then.[13]

Does this mean that children should see, almost as soon as they see anything, a father or a mother on their knees at prayer? Prayer beside young children and prayers with young children would seem the logical way to prepare them for individual prayers on their own. Again, for Christian parents this may involve a whole new range of questions for themselves about what they have to say to God and how they have to say it. Will the prayers that they learned at their mother's knee express what they want to say to God at the cradle of their own sleeping child? Will it carry the whole new understanding of life and work and other lives and other babies that has now come to be of ultimate concern? Here is a severe test of the reality of the parent's own prayer and understanding of God.

So far, we have only considered example, and not precept. It still remains to ask whether children should be given a prayer to say and a suggested time to say it, as a beginning to some kind of disciplined devotional life. At a time when there is a reaction among many who find that prayer has gone dead on them and remains a discipline without profit, this is a particularly difficult question. The two prevailing points of view have been interestingly put by Bishop John Robinson in *Honest to God*, and C. S. Lewis in *Letters to Malcolm*, and a brief résumé of what they have to say will show the opposition between them.

The bishop makes the point:

> If I had the courage, I would start the other end in teaching the discipline of prayer – not from *chronos*, time set by the clock, but from *kairos*, waiting for the moment that drives us to our knees. I am only too conscious that this is dangerous doctrine and that the casualties may be many – though would they be more numerous than those of our present methods? Such an approach requires greater self-discipline, not less. But before it is dismissed as the laxest of all rules of life, I would urge a comparison. There are those who keep fit, and feel they can only keep fit, by a rigid 'constitutional' each day; there are others who reckon to keep in trim by using their common sense, taking exercise as and when they really feel they need it. . . . Our Victorian grandparents believed in the constitutional, in the time-table, and above all in keeping accounts, almost as religiously as some priests now prescribe a rule of life. But one wonders whether there may not for some types be as much liberation in their abandonment as in their observance, and in the end no less discipline.[14]

C. S. Lewis approaches the whole question differently. He does not expect prayer to be pleasant or easy, or always to carry immediate blessing with it:

> I am not therefore deeply moved by the fact that prayer is at present a duty and even an irksome one. This is humiliating. It is frustrating, but we are still only at school. . . . The altar must often be built in one place in order that the fire from heaven may descend somewhere else.[15]

Here the argument would seem to be that, without *chronos*, it is not likely that anything can be expected in the *kairos*.

Both Lewis and Robinson are thinking above all of the adult frustrated with his own failure in prayer. But need children in fact feel this frustration? Is it not possible to lead them from joining in the family prayers to reading some of the modern meditation prayers at night and from these two sources work towards real prayers of their own? Surely the experiment is at least worth trying again.

The same kind of pattern as the contrast between Bishop John Robinson and C. S. Lewis can be found in the churches. Some have done nothing about their children and prayer and have comforted themselves with a text out of its setting which they try to apply: 'When the time comes, the Holy Spirit will instruct you what to say' (Luke 12.12). The result is that some children have found no words to utter, either their own or anyone else's. Equally wrong is the teaching of a set prayer as the only prayer. When this is never grown out of, it cramps development of prayer life and the finding of words to match new experiences. Yet we must never forget that sometimes even this relic of early discipline is the prayer which men and women do use in crises, and when they do, it really expresses feelings which go far beyond the actual words used. Nor is it fair to call this practice a resort to some kind of magical formula. It can be like taking up a conversation once held, which the old words somehow serve to make real again.

Of course, the best prayers will be those in which young people find their own words to express their own feelings and their own reflections on what happens and should happen in human life, directed to One who has shared it in his Son. But the vocalization by others of experiences known and recognizable to the child is not impossible, and may serve as a beginning. From this the child's own thinking may take him on, like Albert Schweitzer, who wondered why he should only be taught to pray for human beings and came to include in his own prayer a prayer for animals because he believed that God was interested in them and loved them as well.

From what has been said here, it will be seen that a special responsibility rests upon parents, a responsibility which, as has been remarked, will be solved not by manuals but by motivation. The reality of worship and prayer at home and in the larger groups to which the children go is of supreme importance. It cannot make the children worship, but it can make them take the whole enterprise seriously, especially when they see that common worship and private prayer are concerned with common life and with the individuals who make up society, the brothers for whom Christ died.

NOTES

1. Iris Murdoch, *The Red and the Green*, Penguin edition, pp. 8 f.
2. J. A. T. Robinson, *Liturgy Coming to Life*, Oxford 1960, p. 22.
3. R. Peil, *A Handbook of the Liturgy*, London 1960, pp. 115 f.
4. Trevor Rowe, in John M. Waterhouse (ed.), *Beware the Church*, London 1968.
5. J. J. von Allmen, *Worship*, p. 28.
6. J. A. T. Robinson, *The New Reformation?*, London 1965, p. 84.
7. Albert H. van den Heuvel, *The Humiliation of the Church*, London 1967, p. 89.
8. R. S. Lee, *Psychology and Worship*, London 1955, pp. 38, 41.
9. J. A. Jungmann, *Handing on the Faith*, London 1959, p. 297.
10. J. A. T. Robinson, *The New Reformation?*, p. 84.
11. Baroness Tweedsmuir, *The Lilac and the Rose*, London 1952, p. 125.
12. Albert H. van de Heuvel, *The Humiliation of the Church*, p. 88.
13. Joyce Kenwrick, *The Religious Quest*, p. 39.
14. J. A. T. Robinson, *Honest to God*, London 1963, p. 103.
15. C. S. Lewis, *Letters to Malcolm: Chiefly on Prayer*, London 1966, p. 150.

5 Learning to Obey

There is a children's hymn which begins:

> Saviour, teach me day by day,
> Love's sweet lesson to obey,
> Sweeter lesson cannot be
> Loving him who first loved me.

The sentiment is impeccable, and fits in with the position outlined in Chapter 2, where Christian obedience was mentioned as a part of the 'given' of any Christian nurture. Here obedience is rightly related to the loving action of God, witnessed to in the Bible and in worship, the response to which is obedience in love. It all seems so essentially right and so essentially simple and uncomplicated.

But Christians will have discovered from any recent reading about Christian ethics that it is apparently far from simple. Moreover, the difficulties mentioned there may have been verified in their own experience, as they have sought to answer the question of the kind of loving response that is required of them in issues of personal and social moral action in the world today. Again, naturally they begin to ask 'What about the children?', and to enquire how more help can be provided for the new generation in the church than was apparently given to their own. This attitude may have been intensified by the fact that the landmarks by which they had hoped to steer their own course are being removed or questioned by society at large and even within the church itself. The parents among them find themselves in the position of those of whom Hebrews writes:

> For indeed, though by this time you ought to be teachers, you need someone to teach you the ABC of God's oracles over again. (Heb. 5.12, NEB.)

Before the question 'What about the children?' can be answered, it may be necessary to start with a quite different question and ask where Christians claim to find guidance to govern their relations with each other, with men and women outside the Christian community, with institutions other than the church and with the whole complex life of society. Such an enquiry in turn may be able to cast some light on how this guidance – if this is the best word for it – can be mediated to the children. (Perhaps 'guidance' here might be understood as a shorthand expression for 'how to respond in love'.)

There are, roughly speaking, three positions which Christians have held about the relation of their faith to the decisions which they take as servants of Christ in the ordinary business of everyday living. A brief examination of each of these is necessary for clarification.

'Prayer ethics'

This term is used to describe an approach to Christian ethics in which guidance is sought as to what the Lord requires either by prayer or some kind of meditation which may be linked with the reading of the Bible. The spoken or unspoken question is, 'Lord, what wouldest Thou have me to do?'. The answer comes by the way of divine inspiration which some claim to have received through the hearing of actual words and others believe to be given in some other way, which none the less declares what course should be taken. The method can be used by individuals or by groups, and the conviction is that the decision is 'given': 'The Lord God showed me.'

One example of this approach today can be found in the Moral Rearmament movement, which has a doctrine of daily guidance by 'spiritual power' to right and wrong actions and causes. They believe that they have the power of the Spirit to tell them daily in a special way what the good is.[1] It would be wrong not to take seriously this attitude of 'Take it to the Lord in prayer', and to dismiss it as an escape from thought or see its only possible result as being the confirmation of the petitioner in a line of action already preferred for other reasons and now appearing to have divine support. Many Christians who witness to the experiences mentioned above go after thought and with minds that are neither completely blank nor completely made up. What they claim to receive is a re-structuring or a resolving of the situation such as they were unable to achieve unaided.

Perhaps it might not be too much to take the Gospel accounts of Jesus' agony in the garden as a picture of what such prayer ethics can be like, and, moreover, presenting an instance where the natural inclination is not supported, but overcome. However, the group manifestations of this approach are easier to describe than the individual cases. Christians regularly open the meetings of their church courts and assemblies with prayer, and believe that their deliberations will be guided by the Holy Spirit. To take another instance from the Bible, one cannot imagine that there was only discussion and no prayer at the Council of Jerusalem, and that the prayer was not a factor in writing the letter which afterwards went to the Gentile churches, which opened: 'It is the decision of the Holy Spirit and our decision . . .' (Acts 15.28). Those who were present at the meeting did not feel that their common mind could have been achieved by common consent alone, but only by all following where the Spirit led.

A variant of this approach in our own time has been called 'instant ethics', where the Spirit is believed to give the Christian the answer along with the situation, declaring the only way to be followed. The Spirit in that case is not 'out there', able from a position of detachment to show what the Lord requires of his puzzled petitioner; the Spirit is 'in there', and showing the seeker what decision he must make.

Reflection shows that this point of view in both of its forms seems to apply mainly to the experiences of crises in life, and scarcely covers that almost unconscious obedience which is offered for a great deal of a person's life, and offered without any request for special help; God is not even specially seen as being directly involved. In such situations, obedience results because of what Christians are or because of what they have become, and willing God's will is more the atmosphere which they breathe than a conscious endeavour to find out what he intends.

'Rule ethics'

A second position begins from the assumption that the Bible is the supreme rule of faith and life, and goes on to assume that the supreme rule is worked out in a series of component rules. The Bible itself can be used to support this position; the Ten Commandments and the Sermon on the Mount have often been cited as suitable rules to guide the Christian life. Earlier generations used the Book of Proverbs for a similar purpose. Jerome, giving advice on the education of Paula, writes: 'Let her gather the rules of life out of the Proverbs of Solomon.' The 'command of the Lord' (I Cor. 7.25), according to the letters of Paul, can be regarded as the supreme ruling, but cases can arise when there are no instructions from the Lord. This, of course, happens more and more as history progresses and societies change. New problems appear which are not dealt with by any specific rulings contained in the Bible.

Where this happens, the method is to find a rule which can be modified to fit or to make some particular deduction from a general rule in order to make it apply. Augustine offers an *outré* example of this: he turns the saying 'Compel them to come in', from the parable of the great feast (Luke 14.23), into a justification for forcible conversion. There are many other instances in which words of the Bible have been equally distorted to serve the cause of casuistry.

This extension of rule-observance into the making of new rules looks very like what Jesus condemned in the Pharisees, when he remarked that they were transgressing the commandments of God for the sake of their own tradition (Matt. 15.2). Nor does it seem to fit with Jesus' own attitude towards the rules, although, as in the case of the sabbath law, he claims that he is doing what the Law intends (see Matt. 12.1 ff.).

On the other hand, it would be wrong only to see what is negative in this approach and to look with the eyes of Paul on the burden of rules when they cannot be kept. Behind this respect for rules is the firm belief that God has made his will known and that he does show his people the way which they should take. It certainly cannot be said that fear of hell was in the past the only motive for keeping the rules. To understand the law of God as he had demonstrated it made his commands attractive ones. It was the God of Abraham, Isaac and Jacob, the God of the Exodus, who commanded. It was not a harsh master, but the God and Father of the Lord and Saviour Jesus Christ who was to be obeyed. Many Christians in the past, and even now, could sing with the Psalmist:

> Meditating all day on your Law,
> how I have come to love it!

> By your commandment, ever mine,
>> how much wiser you have made me than my enemies!
> How much subtler than my teachers,
>> through my meditating on your decrees!
> How much more perceptive than the elders,
>> as a result of my respecting your precepts!
>> (Psalm 119. 97–100, Jerusalem Bible)

When this attitude to the rules is despised, what is often forgotten is that such putting of oneself under the yoke is also an act of free choice. This is neatly expressed in a phrase from the quotation above, 'Your commandment, ever mine'. Much more serious, however, is the criticism that when this is regarded as 'the decision to end all decisions', the rules are never thought about again.

'Love ethics'

This third approach was summed up by Augustine in the famous words, 'Love God and do what you will'. This does not, of course, mean that one does what one likes; it rather claims that a genuine love of God will inevitably result in doing what God's will is, that is, loving. Such a way of looking at obedience fascinates Christians today because it seems to them to embody the very heart of the Gospel and yet to offer a freedom in action which does not deny what God wills or what man is capable of. Such a fresh approach is all the more necessary, it is thought, in times of rapid social change when new situations are continually arising and when the rules seem to apply to them less and less. The effective question then becomes, How shall I show love in this particular situation? Of course, love here is not unrefined or undefined. It is the kind of love that was incarnate in Jesus. His own action shows what love would do, his teaching gives examples of what loving might mean in specific situations (like carrying a Roman soldier's equipment further than was necessary).

87

His parables make their hearers think what harms love or helps it. It is love of this kind and quality, then, that his followers are called on to show:

> To that you were called because Christ suffered on your behalf and thereby left you an example; it is for you to follow in his steps.
> (I Peter 2.20, NEB.)

In a critique of the chapter in *Honest to God* dealing with the new morality, Paul Ramsey sums a position of this kind up in the following way:

> Love alone is the standard because love has a built-in moral compass enabling it to home immediately upon the needs of the other (note well!) in the singleness of the moment of the encounter with him.[2]

The ethic of love is obviously connected with 'situation ethics', the approach based on the principle that 'circumstances alter cases'. It emphasizes the two poles of action, the love to be shown and the particular situation in which it is to be shown, and how these two necessarily influence each other. So what might be a genuine act of Christian love to occupying Roman troops in first-century Jerusalem might not be, if the same were done to occupying Russian troops in twentieth-century Prague.

There is, of course, much to be said for this kind of ethic, but those who discuss it tend to concentrate on exceptions that will prove their rule, in their desire to show how rules can confuse, rather than guide, loving. Take, for instance, the case study in 'sacrificial adultery' given by Joseph Fletcher:

> As the Russian armies drove westward to meet the Americans and British at the Elbe, a Soviet patrol picked up a Mrs Bergmeier foraging food for her three children. Unable to get word to the children, and without any clear reason for it, she was taken off to a prison camp in the Ukraine. . . . The rest of the family never stopped searching. She more than anything else was needed to reknit them as a family in that dire situation of hunger, chaos and fear.

Meanwhile, in the Ukraine, Mrs Bergmeier learned through a sympathetic commandant that her husband and family were trying to keep together and find her. But the rules allowed them to release her for only two reasons: (1) illness needing medical facilities beyond the camp's, in which case she would be sent to a Soviet hospital elsewhere, and (2) pregnancy, in which case she would be returned to Germany as a liability.

She turned things over in her mind and finally asked a friendly Volga German guard to impregnate her, which he did. Her condition being medically verified, she was sent back to Berlin and to her family. They welcomed her with open arms, even when she told them how she had managed it. When the child was born, they loved him more than all the rest, on the view that little Dietrich had done more for them than anybody. . . .

Had Mrs Bergmeier done a good and right thing?[3]

Dietrich Bonhoeffer also recognizes that sometimes loving will mean a suspension of the rules:

For the sake of God and of our neighbour, and that means for the sake of Christ, there is a freedom from the keeping holy of the sabbath, from the honouring of our parents, and indeed from the whole of the divine law, a freedom which breaks this law.[4]

But he goes on to add, 'but only in order to give effect to it anew'. A breach of the law must be recognized in all its gravity.

The nature of Christian obedience

The three approaches outlined above and their variations offer simplified models of the way in which Christians seek to relate faith to life and to find the way of God and do it. All have in common the acknowledgment that the Christian is under some kind of authority, whether external or internalized: 'for Christ did not please himself' (Rom. 15.3). Each knows its failure, the message received and disobeyed, failure to keep the rules when they did apply, self-love rather than love to neighbour arising out of the situation. Yet these frustrations and failures are accepted as part of the Christian realism about man, who is not God and never can be. Nothing alters the fundamental premise that declares that obedience not given is to be deplored or, in religious terms, repented. The engagement, however, is still on.

More positively, when all goes as it should, the Christian feels that the result is of the Lord and not of his own cleverness or faithfulness. Both these positions temper even the most legalistic-seeming approaches to Christian obedience and transform the whole into personal relationships where he who commands and those who obey and those who are the objects of the command and the obedience are all bound together in one bundle of life:

> All are involved in 'What God is doing to make and keep human life human in the world'.[5]

To put it another way, it is a sense of Christ alive and in the midst that prevents the Sermon on the Mount from becoming a new law, except for those who deny that he has lived or does live, and yet approve of 'the Christian ethic'.

With all these considerations as the necessary background, we can now attempt our special question, the way in which children can be trained to recognize and to do what the Lord requires of them, as already members of his church.

Formation through Christ

The starting point for the child in learning to obey is the very fact of his inclusion in the body of Christ through membership of his Christian family and of some particular congregation or house church. Here will be achieved formation, in the sense in which Dietrich Bonhoeffer wishes to use the word:

> It is not a question of applying directly to the world the teaching of Christ or what are referred to as Christian principles, so that

the world might be formed in accordance with these. On the contrary, formation comes only by being drawn in into the form of Jesus Christ. It comes only as formation in his likeness, as *conformation* with the unique form of him who was made man, was crucified, and rose again.

This is not achieved by dint of efforts 'to become like Jesus', which is the way in which we usually interpret it. It is achieved only when the form of Jesus Christ itself works upon us in such a manner that it moulds our form in its own likeness.[6] (Gal. 4.19)

Such thinking recalls our earlier understanding of nurture in terms of the symbols of growth, the vine and the olive, and the results of such growth, which no law can produce:

The harvest of the spirit is love, joy, peace, patience, kindness, goodness, fidelity, gentleness and self-control. There is no law dealing with such things as these. (Gal. 5.22, NEB.)

For many, the difficulty is to recognize the form of Christ in the local congregation and so to believe that the children can be formed by this means:

There can be no absolute confidence that just because one is being nurtured in a community identified as the Body of Christ, only grace will be communicated. Sin also may be learned.[7]

The truth is that the 'shape of Christ' is a 'given' which has yet to be received. So Paul writes to the Galatians:

I am in travail with you over again until you take the shape of Christ. (Gal. 4.19, NEB.)

Christians are summoned to be what they are. So the Corinthians, for all their faults, are God's people at Corinth. May it not be that the very anxiety of Christians for their children's obedience will cause them to reconsider the meaning of their own membership of the body of Christ in the world, as denominations or congregations or Christian families. Such reconsideration might mean a rediscovery that the marks of the church are not the holy marks, the word, the worship and the sacraments, although these are none the less real marks, but the visible doing of the Father's will by loving the world in visible acts of love? The phrase used by the Reformers about the church, *Reformata reformanda*, 'the reformed that is still in need of reform, should be the motto of all churches where children are. They can only achieve this as they produce to the world in word and deed the spirit of the text, 'I am among you like a servant' (Luke 22.27).

Earlier chapters have suggested ways to help children find Christ as prophet speaking through Scripture, Christ as priest in the context of worship. But Christ is only known as king through subjects who obey and make the king and his rule real to the world. Formation by Christ is not independent of the witness of church members and teachers and parents who need specially to be reminded here, 'Become what you are', as a part answer to the question 'What about the children?' This is why a suggestion like Helmut Thielicke's for the establishment of parents' groups within the local congregation is of such practical importance. He writes:

> Through the situation of parenthood we would have in these groups the correlation of the question implied in the situation. . . with the answers implied in the message. The church would then gather a group of people who are really living in the midst of life, who are therefore what we call 'historical people'. . . . In these groups it is impossible to speak docetically. . . . Here I am compelled to deal with the detail, the practical, concrete issues of life and the Word must become flesh.[8]

The responsibilities of parents here are of lasting importance, and psychologists join with theologians in declaring that only in an atmosphere of love and trust can outgoing love begin to take root and grow. Then Christ *is* being formed, and taking shape.

Vocation

A second general preparation for the life of obedience is

the sense of vocation, a word with its own history in Christian thought and used here in Bonhoeffer's sense:

> The calling is the call of Jesus Christ to belong wholly to him. Obedience then is to be tested in 'the total response of the whole man to the whole of reality'.[9]

The child, too, is called of Jesus Christ and what he has to grow into is the sense of commitment to Christ in the whole business of living, not merely in churchly activities nor even only in his secular occupation when he adopts one, as though obedience here could be confined to certain areas, as some of the Reformers thought. In that case, the real world would belong to things indifferent, to which he would not be called, where he need make no decision and take no action.

This must involve a difficult second stage from unconscious assimilation of habits of obedience and even learning and keeping some rule, to a stage beyond, where the radical nature of what is required will become apparent. The analogy of marriage is a useful one here. Mutual love and affection lead to a union in which the total meaning of such a commitment has to be worked out against a background of daily changing circumstances, leading to the discovery:

> There is nothing love cannot face, there is no limit to its faith, its hope and its endurance. (I Cor. 13.7, NEB.)

Formation and vocation together give a general view of the two parts of the process of learning to obey: the formation into the likeness of the one who alone is obedient as he works in the members of his body, and the understanding and the acceptance of vocation as a total commitment to obey. Each of these will now be related to the conscious efforts which the Christian community can make to co-operate in their realization.

93

For the children, there will be what can still be described
as 'learning the rules'. This will be affected by a sort of
conditioning or socialization or indoctrination, all words
which can be used in a good sense, meaning the habit
formation which is part of all good nurture, and not of
Christian nurture alone. In this case, however, such habits
should have their basis in what the adult members of the
church community see for themselves as the obedience
which they offer to Christ and as the love in return which
complements their understanding of the love which has
been shown them in Christ. While example will play its
part, so will precept. The precepts, however, must be such
that those who pass them on to their children are themselves obedient to them. At the earlier stages of child
development they will not need explanation, for the
explanation would scarcely be understood, although the
change in this process can come sooner than later in certain
obvious instances – like not touching the fire because it
burns. Karl Barth asks:

> Where is the line of demarcation between the small and developing
> child? And what child is so small that it may rightly be required
> to behave merely as the object of parental wishes? How can a true
> leading to God's command, and therefore to genuine and personal
> obedience, consent merely in its adjustment to a submission imposed
> from without?[10]

He therefore urges the need to appeal early to freedom
and responsibility, as well as to point to the jurisdiction of
God himself.

How this is to be done is more difficult, and means more
than including God with the parental request in the way
which makes so much of the teaching of Scripture frustrate
its true end. It may be that the encouragement of freedom
and responsibility can be left to the ingenuity of Barth's

'clever mother' or even a clever father. Nonetheless, there should be background teaching from the Bible about people who do what God wants them to do and stories about their modern followers, to help the children to connect, as they are able, some of the things they are told to do with the faithful reasons which lie behind such actions and attitudes. Teaching about Jesus is obviously quite central here. The rules considered earlier, like the Ten Commandments and the Sermon on the Mount, will come to be taught in context as how God wishes people to live together rather than in the analytic way that the Ten Commandments are treated in some of the catechisms. Teaching needs always to be positive. Even when the particular expression is couched in the form of 'Thou shalt not', the commandment must be shown to arise from God's concern for man's good.

If such an approach is adopted, it will itself offer a beginning towards understanding the reason for the rules, so that at least by adolescence the use and limitation of the rules can begin to be established. Their descriptive nature can later be seen as an aid towards identifying the attitudes which show a concern like God's own, although sometimes the rule can be kept without the concern really being shown. The rules can be tested, too, against real or imaginary situations. In his *Teenage Religion*, for example, Harold Loukes provides a 'problem syllabus' in which this whole question can be approached from the actual experience of the adolescent. An analysis of friendship, sex, snobbery, money, work, leisure, prayer, suffering or death can be linked up with passages of the Bible (or parts of the Christian tradition) which have a bearing on these questions.[11] The method has the great virtue of starting young people talking in relation to problems of morals which might well be their own. In such a setting the Bible comes to be used for guidance in a quite new way, and passages other than the obviously ethical may be the most fruitful and helpful in affording insights into moral decision.

An extension of this with older and more able children would be to look at what the Bible says about a particular topic, like those listed above, and follow through the way in which Christians down the ages have looked at the question. In the case of money, for example, study might be made of Clement of Alexandria, *The Rich Man's Salvation*; St Thomas Aquinas, *On Usury*; John Wesley, *The Use of Money*. Nor should imaginative passages like the one quoted from D. H. Lawrence on pp. 41f. be forgotten. Reflection of this kind seems to afford a help towards understanding that the rules define in a general way a 'style of life' which should characterize the conduct of Christians in all kinds of different situations, and even through seemingly different decisions.

The rules, then, are ways of looking at life which have been given by God to his people more as compass than as map. They open up situations rather than define them precisely and show that a decision has to be made, rather than indicating what the decision is. This point might be illustrated from Bonhoeffer's discussion of 'telling the truth':

'Telling the truth' means something different according to the particular situation in which one stands. Account must be taken of one's relationships at each particular time. The question must be asked whether and in what way a man is entitled to demand truthful speech of others. Speech between parents and children is, in the nature of the case, different from speech between man and wife, between friends, between teacher and pupil, government and subject, friend and foe, and in each case the truth which this speech conveys is also different. . . .

'Telling the truth', therefore, is not solely a matter of moral character; it is also a matter of correct appreciation of real situations and of serious reflection upon them. The more complex the actual situations of a man's life, the more responsible and the more difficult will be his task of 'telling the truth'. The child stands in only one vital relationship, his relationship to his parents, and he, therefore, still has nothing to consider and weigh up. The next environment in which he is placed, the school, already brings with it the first difficulty. From the educational point of view it is, therefore, of the very greatest importance that parents . . . should make their children understand the differences between these various circles in which they are to live and the differences in their responsibilities.[12]

As a result, telling the truth is 'something which must be learnt'. Again, as with the Bible and prayer, the guiding and teaching here cannot ensure the obedience which it would wish to effect. At best, it can commend it and exemplify it, and hope that the result will be a desire to 'go and do likewise'.

Before this can happen, there must be an acknowledgment of formation and a confession of vocation. The spirit of what this implies is summed up in the prayer said by a Bar-Mitzvah, a boy when he is said to be morally responsible and is admitted into the Jewish community:

O my God and God of my fathers, on this solemn and sacred day which marks my passage from boyhood to manhood, I humbly raise my eyes unto thee and declare with sincerity and truth that henceforth I will keep thy commandments and undertake and bear the responsibility of mine actions toward thee. In my earliest infancy I was brought within thy sacred covenant with Israel and today I again enter as a responsible member, the elect congregation in the midst of which I will not cease to proclaim thy holy name in the face of all nations.[13]

As was already suggested, this will not be 'the decision to end all decisions', but a recognition of the way in which all decisions will be taken. Nor will it mean that the decisions of the fathers will necessarily be binding on the children. Karl Barth recognizes how the development of freedom and responsibility can make the child 'stand on his own feet and face his parents'. His obedience to God will not always be shown in their ways. He will ask his own questions in his own situation, 'What am I as a Christian to do?'.

Group decisions

The very recognition of the individualism of this question, 'What am I as a Christian to do?', in the setting of the relation between the generations, raises once more the need to ask what place group decision may have in obedience. This seems to have characterized some of the situations in the early church. Paul's letters are intended to help groups of Christians on decisions which they must take, and to help them to learn to obey. Most remarkable is the Epistle to Philemon, which is addressed to the church as well as to Philemon, as if what happened to Onesimus was a matter for them all, although Philemon was the most nearly concerned. There does seem to be a need in the church for groups which do concern themselves with particular matters of Christian obedience, like the group mentioned by Horst Symanowski:

> When universal military training was proclaimed in East Germany in January 1962, six young married couples who met regularly as a 'house church' discussed the meaning of this law for themselves and their companions. The latter had immediately begun to ask them what they ought to say and what their attitude should be in the face of this issue. Some of them had given various answers, although all of them seemed inadequate at that moment. Some of them had remained silent. What did Jesus Christ demand of them in that situation?[14]

In such groups, the way of obedience would be learned incarnationally and not docetically, to repeat Thielicke's phrase (see above, p. 92), and a new solidarity of community in obedience achieved to answer the question, 'What are we as the people of God in this place to do?' It may be that young people will have the revelation which older people need and cannot find:

Parents lose a lot of imagination as they grow older and become more materialistic. . . . But parents have great things to offer.[15]

These two remarks from a report of a discussion group of older teenagers on parents show both the need and the opportunity for more coming together to find the way in which the Lord wishes all to take in his service. One can imagine the benefit of the Ten Commandments being discussed in such a group of younger and older people. In such groups, one of the positive contributions of situation ethics might be put into practice, the need to search out and master the facts of any situation where difficult decisions need to be taken. It is all too easy to find New Testament solutions that will not stand up to newspaper facts or to more sober information which takes more effort to search out for oneself. Indeed, this applies to all the ethical thinking which we expect young people to do, and is one way of helping them to see if their solutions are applicable to the real problems. After all, there was more in the case of Onesimus than to have him back; there was the whole question of the law and the possible effect on other masters and slaves, as well as the family affair aspect of the case within the Christian community.

Action and attitude

So far, learning to obey, apart from what was said about disciplining at the beginning, seems largely to have been a commendation of talk, however enlightened and relevant talk it might be. But obedience has really to do with action and attitude. Therefore, learning to obey should be more like learning a skill than mastering information. Interestingly enough, this point of view is expressed quite often in writing concerned with moral education, for example: 'the learning may be a learning of skills rather than facts'. It can come about 'through the promotion of good activities'.

99

One book has been given the title *Christian Education as Engagement*,[16] because the author feels that the use of the word 'education' has put a wrong emphasis on what the church has to offer to children and young people. Education suggests the supplying of information, while engagement suggests encounter, in this case both with God and with the neighbour. Here is a concept much nearer to all that is implied by the New Testament command 'to make disciples'.

The schools themselves are moving rapidly in the direction of participation and learning by doing, but the church has been slow to follow them except in the externals of this movement. It may be because this is so difficult a thing to do in the moral field, to give the experience of a good deed or a kind act, if it is really possible at all. Yet, as the hymn which opened this chapter reminded us, 'Love in loving finds employ'. But can it be devised or structured to give the feel of what love is like, or what love will imply?

At the older ages it may be less difficult, because there children can plan their own deeds of love and carry them through. Many Christian groups of young people could tell how they have found for themselves what loving means and what loving costs, when it is carried out, not in one impulsive gesture, but in a continuous duty which seems to bring no immediate reward or understanding with it. Yet experiments are possible with younger children, and two examples of how such experiments have been made or might be made are given here for clarification. The first was a Sunday School experiment with quite young children who were asked to bring a favourite toy to Sunday School and then to let other children play with it. Here is a primary experiment in learning the skill of sharing and sacrifice at the simplest level, and yet which does confront the child with a real decision. Another might be devised from the need to help children from about nine onwards, to learn the stewardship of money. The Christian way of life both in Scripture and tradition is obviously concerned with this quite real problem. Aquinas and Calvin show a similar realization of the difficulty of knowing what to keep for oneself and what to give to brothers in need. Yet how seldom are children given a sense of money and helped to budget with it, even when they are handling money provided for various enterprises, from church collections to sweets, from subscriptions to charitable appeals made at school to money for 'the pictures'. This teaches nothing about how money should be spent; merely to dole out the sums required is less helpful than giving some kind of allowance and giving some time to discuss how and why it might be spent.

Love to a neighbour does not come sharply to life only by taking the church flowers to an old lady. No one would wish children to carry more than they are able to bear, but there is need for much more imaginative enquiry into good ways of disciplining into obedience which will show the fulfilment and the frustration which this involves, and the failure, too. It may be that those new situations which some churches are devising for young children on their first coming to church, and the training which they are offering to those who will look after them there, are creating true schools of faith where real caring can be learned and good personal relations promoted. The present tendency of some in the church to get this stage over quickly, so that more conventional teaching and learning may begin, is therefore to be regretted, if it prevents the extension of the experiments with the younger children in appropriate ways into the older groups. For learning at depth in Christian terms can come about in this way. 'Whoever has the will to do the will of God shall know whether my teaching comes from him or is merely my own' (John 7.17, NEB).

Obedience and prayer

There still remains one more aspect of the way in which Christians seek to learn to do the will of God, and its relevance for children – the sincerely held belief that prayer has a place in ascertaining what God would have men do. Is this to be taught to children, too? Nothing could be more provoking in a situation where advice or discussion of difficulty is sought and the only answer given is, 'Go away and pray about it'. It would seem that the approach with children to the place of prayer in ethical guidance should never be made by direct teaching of this sort. Rather, they should come to understand through public and group prayer that God is concerned with what happens in the world and with the decisions which his children are called upon to make. If children are able to take part in congregational action groups which begin and end their discussions with relevant prayer, then they can begin to understand their problems in a new frame of reference, realizing that Christ, too, is in the very situation which is calling for some specific response of love. In this way they can best learn that prayer is not a device to persuade Christ to take an interest or to do away with the need to think what love should or should not do. Rather, it is a way to put them on his side and to help them to see the situation through his eyes. From such experience of group prayer in the ethical area, their own individual prayers are most likely to arise.

This is only the barest sketch of an urgent and pressing aspect of nurture where the old assurance of the 'given' as 'the law in ordinances' is being replaced by a feeling that 'the letter kills, but the Spirit makes alive'. The stage-by-stage approach to inducting children into obedience as a conscious co-operation of men as well as the free action of the Spirit still awaits more study and more experiment. The one encouraging fact is that those who investigate the whole question of moral education apart from religion are equally tentative in their conclusions, and equally sensitive to the need to find new and better methods.

NOTES

1. Joseph Fletcher, *Situation Ethics*, London 1966, p. 24.
2. Paul Ramsey, *Deeds and Rules in Christian Ethics* (enlarged edition), New York 1967, p. 23.
3. Joseph Fletcher, *Situation Ethics*, pp. 164 f.
4. Dietrich Bonhoeffer, *Ethics*, London 1955, p. 229.
5. Paul Lehmann, *Ethics in a Christian Context*, London 1963, p. 99.
6. Dietrich Bonhoeffer, *Ethics*, p. 18.
7. R. R. Boehlke, *Theories of Learning in Christian Education*, Philadelphia 1962, p. 122.
8. Helmut Thielicke, *The Trouble with the Church*, London 1966, p. 119.
9. Dietrich Bonhoeffer, *Ethics*, p. 225.
10. Karl Barth, *Church Dogmatics*, III, 4, Edinburgh 1961, p. 251.
11. Harold Loukes, *Teenage Religion*, ch. V. See also Douglas Rhymes, *Prayer in the Secular City*, Appendix I.
12. Dietrich Bonhoeffer, *Ethics*, pp. 326 f.
13. *Authorized Daily Prayerbook of the United Hebrew Congregations of the British Empire*, p. 302.
14. Horst Symanowski, *The Christian Witness in an Industrial Society*, London 1964, p. 84.
15. P. Jephcott, *Time of One's Own*, Edinburgh 1967, p. 87.
16. David Hunter, *Christian Education as Engagement*, New York 1963.

6 Turning Athens into Jerusalem

What is there in common between Athens and Jerusalem? What between the Academy and the Church? What between heretics and Christians? . . . Away with all projects for a 'Stoic', 'Platonic' or a 'dialectic' Christianity! After Christ Jesus we desire no subtle theories, no acute enquiries after the Gospel.[1]

So writes Tertullian, and seems at one savage blow to demolish the need of the Christian for education other than that which the church provides. His position is all the more interesting today, at least in Britain, because some Christians appear to see school education as the legitimate and necessary extension of Christian nurture, and it is therefore the non-Christian who now asks, 'What is there in common between Athens and Jerusalem?', as he seeks to banish Christianity from the schools. It has been common to speak of home, church and school as the three agencies which most influence the growing child and help in determining what he shall become. Moreover, it is assumed that their aims will always be the same and that no conflict can arise between them.

However, the history of even the last fifty years in Britain shows that this is not so:

Few topics more steadily held national interest in Great Britain at the opening of the twentieth century than the religious issue in State schools. Should schools under the control of the churches receive financial aid from public sources? Should religious instruction be included in the daily timetables of schools? Well known men from all walks of life entered into the heated discussion . . . The immense literature on the subject bears witness to the intensity of the debate.

Newspapers and periodicals carried frequent editorials and articles. The printing presses poured forth a never-ending stream of pamphlets and books. The public forum – demonstrations, parades, meetings, legislative deliberations, yielded a plethora of addresses and speeches. For the people in the British Isles, the controversy provided an emotional excitement not unlike that generated in France by the contemporary Dreyfus affair. The strife produced court trials, prison sentences, distraint of property, election issues, exchanges between opposing church leaders and negotiations in political circles. The nation was in deadly earnest over the adage that 'He who holds the child moulds the man'.[2]

So writes an American researcher into this situation. Nor is the debate over, even if it is not conducted with such vehemence, makes only an occasional second editorial rather than a banner headline, and ranks only a few small pamphlets. It tends now to be the concern of the interested few, although opinion polls seek out from time to time the views of the rather indifferent many. But what is at issue is germane to any discussion which has concerned itself with Christian nurture, and so this chapter must especially concern itself with the relation of Christian nurture to religious education in schools.

A historical survey

To understand the present, it is necessary to survey the past. In spite of Tertullian, the Christian church not only concerned itself with handing on the faith but also showed its concern for handing on knowledge and skills which show the greatness of the human spirit and the possibilities of human enterprise. Religion and learning, however, had to go hand in hand, because learning without religion was cruelly deficient:

Pietas literata – a Christian liberal education was the ideal of Protestant and Catholic alike.[3]

Even where the state, or some other form of authority than the church itself, undertook the task of education, it was

105

still to be 'godly upbringing'. Martin Luther, for example, writes 'To the Councilmen of All Cities in Germany that they Establish and Maintain Christian Schools'. The famous section on schools in the Scottish *First Book of Discipline*, which has been attributed to John Knox, is addressed to 'godly magistrates'. It offers them a blueprint for an educational system which has 'knowledge of the Christian religion' as an integral part; for 'their principles ought and must be learned in the youth heid'.[4] If one believes with Augustine that 'Thou hast made us for thyself, and our hearts are restless till they find their rest in thee', any education where this dimension of life is omitted would be incomplete, and a whole possibility and necessity of human life, and that the most important, would be unexplored.

When the Christian church provided the schools or had the school under its control, the school was as much an extension of the church, sometimes literally and physically so, as the Christian home itself. Church rites and ceremonies were incorporated into the school life, church doctrines were taught, committed teachers witnessed in deed as well as in word. All other learning was consciously or unconsciously related to this essentially Christian disciplining. Both Catholics and Protestants would see value in this position, although not necessarily for the same reasons. The Catholic would perhaps stress the Catholic atmosphere that such a school would offer to the child during his formative years. The Protestant, perhaps more intellectual in his emphasis, would point to the knowledge of the Christian religion which the school was able to supply, to the teaching of reading and the memorizing of the Catechism, both useful tools for informed personal perusal of the Scriptures. For:

> The whole counsel of God concerning all things necessary for his own glory, man's salvation, faith and life, is either expressly set

down in Scripture, or by good and necessary consequence may be deduced from Scripture.[5]

And the schools helped to provide the keys which opened this treasure.

Difficulties, however, begin to arise with the multiplication of denominations which introduce new aims for the school or present the old ones in new forms. Catholic schools come to be valued for their ability to produce committed Catholics. The divisions in Protestantism are reflected in denominational schools which serve the denominations to keep members or recruit them. This, however, was not true in every case. Candlish, a distinguished ecclesiastical statesman of the Free Church of Scotland, when his own church set up schools after the Disruption of 1834, is on record as saying of them:

> We do not plant our schools as nurseries of the Free Church, nor do we ask our teachers to make proselytes of the pupils. Our schools are really as simply and purely elementary schools for giving a good elementary education to the young as were the best Parish schools before the Disruption.[6]

All the churches, however, had the merit of being concerned for general as well as religious and denominational education in their schools.

The main difficulty comes, of course, when the state begins to play a chief part in education, setting up schools at the public expense, making education compulsory for all. This was the situation which produced the Dreyfus-like reaction to which the quotation from Benjamin Sacks refers. The questions were legion. Should church schools continue, and should they be maintained or partly maintained at state expense? Should the new state schools have religion built into the curriculum as had schools of all sorts until now, and if so, what kind of religious teaching should it be? There was fairly general agreement that it should be

Christian, but beyond that, little agreement of what 'Christian' would mean in practice. Bible lessons? Catechisms? Prayers? The whole Bible? Each of these suggestions in turn opened rather than settled a discussion. All were not so complacent as the Aberdeenshire schoolmaster who was asked about the possibility of a national system of education for Scotland:

> My views are distinctly in favour of a national system of education in preference to a denominational system. The tendency of the present age is to split up into sects and parties. This, every one will allow, is not 'for edification'. If the taste for such distinction is fostered in youth, it will certainly increase as years advance. In a national system, with *one set of* machinery, the beneficial results are likely to be more rapid than in a denominational system, where you have *several* sets, and in all probability the one set counteracting the good effects of the other. The Shorter Catechism would suit all parties (the Episcopalian Catechism to be taught when wanted). The Bible and New Testament are also all that any party can demand and these are quite sufficient, I should think. I cannot fancy a reasonable objection to a national system, as regards the subject matter of education, for all Dissenters use the Bible and the Shorter Catechism, except the Episcopalians, and they may easily have their own. The religion of Popery I would condemn; if the children of Roman Catholics did not choose to get another Catechism, they should not be forced. I knew several teachers who have taught children of all denominations and I am aware they never had any difficulty with the religious branch. What is true of one section of the land may be predicted of the whole. When our various denominations sink their *envious feelings*, the *sectarian differences* will crumble of themselves.[7]

Marjorie Cruickshank's book *Church and State in English Education*[8] should be compulsory reading for all who would learn how difficult it is for the state and the church to find acceptable compromises on such issues, even when the prevailing ethos of the state is Christian and Christianity is regarded as the established religion. (Establishment in the sense of an 'established church' further complicated the issue and explains some of the positions taken.) If the state,

108

however, does not uphold one form of Christianity, or what some consider essential to that form (for example creeds or catechisms, or religious feast-days and holidays), it can only commit itself to some general and undenominational Christianity. This was thought to be secured in England by the famous Cowper-Temple clause, which forbade in rate-aided schools the use of 'any catechisms or religious formularies distinctive of any particular denomination'. The later and more positive Agreed Syllabus approach was a means directed to the same end.

The present situation

The present system in England is a compromise: state schools with religious education and religious observance by law established, and church schools with limited support from the state in return for satisfying certain educational demands. Scotland has all state schools, but Catholics (and Episcopalians) can have their own schools with their own special provision for religious education and all at the state's expense – an anomaly between the two parts of the country hard to explain unless the remark made (certainly as far back as 1878) by His Majesty's Inspector of Schools that 'the public schools are to all intents and purposes denominational schools, public and Presbyterian are practically interchangeable', throws some light on the matter.

The compromise seems to require for its justification a belief in some kind of Christendom, albeit a divided and denominational one. Those who are not content with religion in general, as for example Anglicans and Catholics, will pay extra to have that religion in particular which the church school seems to secure to them. Minority dissent in state schools is catered for by the conscience clause, which allows parents who desire no religious education for their children to contract them out. The implication is that the majority is for the *status quo*, and opinion polls like that done by *New Society* would seem to support this opinion:

> If these replies are typical, there is overwhelming support in Britain for the continuance of religious education within the state school system as the educational expression of a society which regards itself, however vaguely, as a Christian country.[9]

The present position is not, however, without its critics. There is a new realism about the increasing pluralistic nature of British society. It is based on the presence in the schools of many children of immigrants whose religion is not Christian, and the determined protest by humanists and others that they neither wish religious education for their children nor are satisfied with the oddness which withdrawal under the conscience clause would confer upon them in the largely conformist school community. There is, too, an increasing feeling on the part of some churchmen that the money the church spends in a never-ending battle on the rising cost of providing church schools would more properly be spent in other activities better related to the church's mission in the world. Bishop John Robinson has this point of view for the Anglicans:

> The Church creates – or more often inherits – specifically ecclesiastical institutions, paralleling rather than permeating the structures of the world. Frequently these are hang-overs from the day when the Church pioneered services where the community at large was failing to provide them. This is notably the case in regard to education in England, where there were no public authority schools till less than a century ago. But I cannot believe that, except in a few cases which could serve as laboratories for fresh experiment, the continuing Christian concern for education is now most meaningfully (let alone economically) expressed by retention of the dual system of church and state schools and training colleges. If a tenth of the money was spent on intensive work with Christian and non-Christian teachers in secular schools and colleges, I believe the Church might get somewhere.[10]

A similar point of view has been put forward for some

Catholics.[11] There is the opinion voiced in many quarters that as the comprehensive school seeks to do away with some of the barriers which divide children, the denominational school perpetuates divisions of another kind, and does so in the name of Christ. But most of all, there is a new interest among educationalists in religious education as belonging to the school in its own right, and not as an extension of the activities of the church.

This educational interest in religion in schools has led to much discussion about the curriculum and the methods which would be appropriate to such a religious education. Much of this thinking about the new religious education is still at the experimental stage, as are the attempts to provide a 'new school worship'.[12] Such a summary description fails to give expression to the genuine heart-searching among educationalists for the best way to include within the school curriculum some enquiry into the deep questions about man and his destiny and duty, and some of the answers which have commonly been given. Nor does it do justice to the thought given about methods to be employed so as to secure enlightenment rather than indoctrination, and yet to promote the desire to experience as well as merely to be informed. All these factors together suggest that changes small or great, are coming.

Moreover, the position is even more complex than it seems. The separation between church school and state school is not absolute. The church is already present in the state school through the presence of teachers and pupils who are members of it. Nor does Christ need to be 'brought' to the state schools (the awful warning implied in Dom Sebastian Moore's story of the industrial chaplain who said, 'I am bringing God into industry'). Christ is already there as he is everywhere that his children need him. The signs of his presence are surely there, for example, in the

111

loving care and concern which so many teachers show to deprived children, so giving them the only love and security which they know. Then, again, the world can exist in the church school in the presence of teachers who are not committed to the things for which the school stands, and in children who have no religious background at all. More subtle still may be the fact that the real values of a church school can sometimes be those of the competitive materialistic society rather than those of its Christian profession. Moreover, from the earliest Christian times, nurture never seems to have been looked upon as an alternative to general education which the church has always regarded as worthwhile in itself as well as valuable for the church's own purpose and mission. Of course, education can be perverted and become demonic, as happened in Nazi Germany, but where it operates on broad and liberal lines the church has welcomed it as a good, always to be related to the Good News which came by Jesus Christ. Christian nurture is never likely to mean that children can dispense with some kind of general education.

Choosing a school

It is in this complex and changing situation that the Christian church and Christian parents who are committed to bring up their children 'in the nurture and admonition of the Lord' must plan their strategy, for the other major influence upon their children will be their school. Their concern will show itself by the school they choose, where they have a choice and, where they have no choice, by the way in which they relate their own Christian nurture to what the school supplies, and the way in which they frame their particular requests to the school. Here it is assumed that the choice will be between church schools and state schools within the public sector. Private schools offer additional choices, but only for the limited number who can pay the fees or whose children can win scholarships to them.

The churches which have church schools obviously must regard these as necessary for their total understanding of what nurture implies. The atmosphere and ethos of such schools should confirm and continue, in a setting different from church and home, what these two are already striving to impart. The value of this for younger children who are at that stage of formation where they are still acquiring the framework from which ultimately their own freedom can come is considerable. Such children are too young, some would say, to be faced with the conflict which they are too immature to resolve. In theory, at least, the church school should provide an environment which is Christian, not only because it includes Christian teaching and worship, but because those who teach the children are men and women of commitment, living out what they teach. The result would be to make all the major influences affecting the child at this stage tend in the same direction, and provide him with the necessary basis for his adventures into a differentiated and different world later on. But even some who would approve of church schools for younger children for this reason are beginning to wonder whether it is wise for children to continue in these after the primary stage.

After this, the effect can be quite the opposite, keeping children from discovering for themselves both through learning and through experience that the environment in which they will ultimately live is not simple and whole; there are other churches, other faiths or no faith, other moral standards, different choices made. Of course, the church school can and should teach about all these things. Its weakness, however, has been that often it has not done so, and has suppressed differences and difficulties. Thus its children met a hostile or indifferent world, unprepared for what they would find there, or else the children themselves recoiled from a meaningless uniformity which seemed to offer no choices at the very time when they were becoming conscious of both freedom and discontent. Moreover, the experience of a mixed community as opposed to teaching about the differences would make the non-church school seem a better preparation for the mixed society where the church's children will live their lives.

One can understand that churches and church parents wish the best for their children, and that the best is to keep them committed to the fellowship in which they are nurtured, but the church school can no more inevitably do this than the church's own procedures for nurture. Whether it is more likely to do so is difficult to establish. Attempts have been made both in Britain and in the United States to do this for Catholic schools, but although many interesting things have emerged, the result would seem to be a cautious 'Not Proven', as both those for and those against have found some support for their arguments in the conclusions.[13] Of course, it could be argued that the school offers a sure shield to protect this early and delicate planting. In all fairness, however, it is not on such negatives that the case for church schools generally rests, nor does it base itself on vague statements about curriculum reminiscent of Dr Pusey's:

> All things must speak of God, refer to God, or they are atheistic. History without God is a chaos without design . . . political economy without God would be a selfish teaching about the acquisition of wealth . . . physics without God would be a dull enquiry into such meaningless phenomena.[14]

Attitudes like this deny the autonomy of the educational disciplines and sometimes have led to a kind of educational censorship very different from a true Christian concern for the truth. The argument really rests on the influence and atmosphere which the church school provides, where all that is taught is assimilated within the framework of belief in and obedience to Jesus Christ. At any rate, the values which some churches and parents attach to church schools is shown by their sacrificial giving to keep these operating, and the willingness of parents to sacrifice some of the amenities and opportunities of state education for the more lasting benefits which the church-orientation of the school seems to afford. Yet, as we have seen, there is a tendency at the moment, proceeding from the ecumenical as well as the secularizing trends of the present time, only to make a case for church schools at the primary stage, and beyond this to consider the possibility of all children, whatever their background, attending the same school.

State schools and the church

The churches, obviously, have some kind of interest (all do not appear to have the same interest) in state schools. This interest has often been expressed mainly in the attempt to see that religion, understood as Christian religion, has its place as part of the curriculum in such schools. By this means, it is believed, an essential link is formed between church and school. Morning prayers in school resemble prayers in church. Religious lessons use mainly the same biblical material as the church employs in its own instruction. Lessons on the church itself and on great Christians are included in the syllabus. More advanced courses will consider biblical and theological and ecumenical problems, and the relation of religion to ethics.

On the whole, such a programme would seem to offer a reinforcement and enlargement of some of the task of church nurture with the advantages of more time, and in some cases, better grouping of pupils, for purposes of study.

Very often, too, the teaching can be given by those who are already themselves committed and therefore interpret the Christian position as standing within it. Perhaps the churches have shown their gratitude for this in a curious way by looking on the state schools as if they were some kind of undenominational church school, like the army's category of 'other denomination' for 'religious allegiance'. Some schools and schoolmasters have interpreted their task in similar terms. But such an attitude provokes a sharp reaction from teachers who are not committed, and raises questions about children who come with a different religious background, or none at all, under the thin protection of the conscience clause.

It is therefore clear new thinking needs to be done about the possibility of a school, even with religious education on the time-table, being regarded as a Christian community, when it more accurately reflects in its teachers and in it pupils the pluralist society of today. Sometimes the recognition of this fact in church circles has only led to the replacement of the Christian community image by a mission-field image. Then the reason for the school's existence is merely to afford an opportunity to the church to reach those children whom it has lost, or perhaps never even had. Both these images are understandable and in some ways commendable. But neither is helpful in the present time. What is required on the part of the churches is a fresh look at the developments which are taking place in religious education within the school context itself, and a real evaluation and consideration of them.

The new curricula and methods will not seem so obviously church-related or Christian-centred. Some of them may involve taking religious education out of its 'special' place as separate and apart from what else is taught. The use of the integrated day in the primary school, for example, will require this if it is to include an element of religion. And

116

what kind of religion will it be, and how will it be presented, if all the children, of all beliefs, are to go through it all together?

At the other end, religious education has been included in a programme of 'Social Studies' in some secondary schools. These approaches imply a new objectivity which will have its difficulties:

> Are we, for example, prepared to have both St Francis and Dr Verwoerd recognized as men who believe themselves to be acting in obedience to the will of God? I do not cite this example because I believe it must somehow shake the faith of persons with religious beliefs, but because I fear there may be many who think that it would, and who will therefore insist that only certain approved and respectable examples of religiously inspired lives can be presented to young children.[15]

Moreover, other religious books than the Bible are likely to be opened in the school, and other religions than Christianity examined. Morality, too, will be looked at from the standpoint of religion, but from other standpoints too. What are the consequences of this likely to be for Christian nurture? On the whole, they could be nothing but good, and may serve to remind the church that its nurture has been less than true when some of these considerations have not been brought to the children's notice at the proper place and time in the church's own situation.

There is an additional value, especially for the adolescent from a church background, in having the familiar looked at in a quite different setting and put in relation to other things. Too often in the past the offering of school and church in religion has had a sameness which led to boredom in both, however well the material was presented. Moreover, there can be help in making young people see that their fathers' faith has to be known and defended and adopted as their own, and that even the same faith can be looked at otherwise (and yet not negatively) than the way in which

117

they have received it. The tragic revelation of Edmund Gosse's *Father and Son* is his assumption that there is only one way of looking at Christianity, his father's.

Another result might be that those responsible for nurture in the church may be faced with eager questions rather than the passivity which they have sometimes encountered. Both school and church would benefit if religious education can come out of the ghetto situation in the school and into the full sweep of the school life, important and interesting for all pupils, irrespective of background and belief. John Wilson has sketched what such an approach to religious education might involve:

> A good deal of what has been given under the heading of 'R.E.' might disappear, but a good deal would remain. The test would be whether what is taught contributed to the education of the emotions in this sphere, and planning experience and understanding not only of Christianity but other religions (and quasi-religions such as Fascism) could so contribute. Experience and an emotional grasp of context of Christian and non-Christian worship would be essential, and, granted our basic aim, would justify some sort of religious assembly in school. But we should also be concerned with the problem from the other end – that is, to help the child to understand and control his existing feelings of awe, guilt and so on, whatever objects they might be directed toward. Our ultimate task is not to ensure that by any means the child ends up by worshipping what he thinks he ought to worship, but to increase the powers of his reason so that he may more rationally decide for himself what, if anything, he should worship.[16]

With such a programme, those who are concerned about the Christian nurture of their children can have no quarrel because they can have no reasonable fear of it. Only those who have confused Athens with Jerusalem and sought to make one after the image of the other will be opposed, Paul at Athens, making his appeal in the market place with its competing voices, is a better guide here to right relations between church nurture and school religious education.

The end of religious education?

One possibility remains which has not yet been discussed: that religious education may disappear from the state schools altogether, as is the practical fact in America and is likely to become a fact in Canada, with the consent of the churches. However unlikely the possibility may be, especially if the subject becomes as liberally understood as John Wilson suggests that it could be, and the arrangements at the school for both worship and instruction made more flexible than they have been sometimes in the past – nonetheless the question must be asked, what might be the consequences for Christian nurture?

An example from the past might help. For the first three centuries, there were no Christian schools to which parents could send their children, for a variety of reasons.

So the Christian small boy in the fourth century was, like his Gentile fellows, copying out the names of pagan gods and learning to read from the same old authors.[17]

More would be involved than the pagan content of the lessons. The school would be organized to fit in with pagan religion. Its holidays would be the feast days of the gods and not the Christian festivals. Only rarely might the teacher of the Christian child himeslf be a Christian. Yet it was in this period that the church grew, according to some authorities, not so much by converting the world as by keeping within the faith those who were born and baptized into the church. At any rate, these early Christians had been convinced that such a pagan education could not destroy what the Christian church and Christian parents continued to give the children. Rather, the one helped them to discriminate in the use of the other. His Christian nurture enabled the Christian child to distinguish the true from the false, useful and useless, in what was offered to

119

him by the school. A similar testimony is borne today by some French Catholics, that attendance at state schools which have no teaching about religious faith has done no real damage, and in some ways has been positive gain for Catholic Christian young people. The same has been said by Protestants in America. In both cases the churches concerned recognize a challenge in this kind of situation to their own attempts at education and to their own understanding of and relation to the state schools where the children go. Both these countries, however, have a different history and tradition from Britain.

Nevertheless, will Christian nurture suffer if ever religion should disappear from the school? Certainly this is not the end, as alarmists sometimes seem to be saying, as far as the church is concerned. It is against the church and not against religion in schools that the gates of hell will not prevail. If it did come to pass, however, churches might wish to establish their own schools, and this is happening in some denominations in America, for whom a school without religion has become meaningless. Churches might want to protest because it would seem educationally wrong to deprive children of such knowledge and experience of a whole area of human life, important even for the understanding of literature and art, of music and history, and even of the origins of science itself. Such a protest, however, is not in order to safeguard nurture, but is a plea for truth. F. R. Barry has a comment which is applicable here:

> If we want to see a revival of religion, Christians ought to be very much concerned with the content of statutory education – to press for the inclusion of subjects which inculcate a sense of depth and mystery and stimulate and foster imagination. But religious and moral values in education are commended not only and perhaps not even mainly through religious channels – the divinity periods or the chapel services. They are given, and almost unconsciously received, through the ethos, tone and tradition of the society – the

aims and standards found to be accepted in it, what it approves and what it disapproves, what qualities it holds most in honour, how its members treat one another, and what would be distinctively Christian here, surely, is respect and reverence for personality, the conviction that people matter more than things, that the system was made for man, not man for the system, that all that is taught and learned has a human purpose – is a preparation for serving human needs, not only a certificate for a good job – and that the object of the entire exercise is the nurture and fulfilment of persons.[18]

Perhaps in Britain the churches have been lulled into security by the apparent correspondence between the aims of education and their own particular aims, by the pastoral care and concern by most teachers of their children, and the enlargement of life which the school can bring. Further, for this the church may take no small credit and may reasonably hope that it will continue. For those who are most vocal against religious education in schools themselves stand for the things which Barry praises and which are generally acceptable in this society as being the marks of the 'good schools'. Christianity claims to have more to offer than this. The churches, however, should not expect the state to make room for this offering against the wishes of the majority in the community, if ever there should be such a majority with such a mind.

The relation of church nurture to school education, as it was and is and may yet be, has been sufficiently ventilated for summary conclusions to be reached. Nurture can be both hindered and helped by what happens in schools, but the help and the hindrance factors are not determined by the simple criteria which are sometimes employed. It may not always happen that the more the school is like the church the more the church children benefit, or that the kind and the quality of the religion in school must correspond with the church's own to be of real use. Most important of all must be the church's attempt to understand the general education given in the schools and its prevailing ethos in relation to what it seeks to do for its own children. It will be in this way that it may best express its concern for those other children whom it wishes to win but cannot ask the school to evangelize on its behalf. It is in this way, too, that there might emerge a real partnership more helpful both to Christian nurture and to Christian evangelism, when the church remembers that its function in relation to the school, as to all other such institutions, is 'one of ministry not of secret lordship'.[19]

NOTES

1. Tertullian, *De Praescriptione Haereticorum* VII, quoted in Bettenson, *Documents of the Christian Church*, p. 8

2. B. Sacks, *The Religious Issue in the State Schools of England and Wales*, Albuquerque 1961, p. 5.

3. Edmund Fuller (ed.), *The Christian Idea of Education*, Yale 1962, p. 64.

4. *First Book of Discipline*, VII, 1, 'Of the Necessity for Schools'.

5. *Westminster Confession of Faith*, 1.6.

6. Quoted by W. Boyd, *Education in Ayrshire through Seven Centuries*, London 1961, p. 133.

7. A. G. Sellar and C. F. Maxwell, *Reports on Education for Scotland*, Edinburgh 1886, pp. 204 f.

8. London 1963.

9. *New Society*, 27 May 1965.

10. J. A. T. Robinson, *The New Reformation?*, p. 94.

11. Bernard Tucker (ed.), *Catholic Education in a Secular Society*, London 1968, p. 2.

12. See e.g. A. R. Bielby, *Sixth Form Worship*, London 1968; *Education Through Worship*, London 1969.

13. A. E. C. W. Spencer, 'An Evaluation of Roman Catholic Educational Policy in England and Wales 1900–1960', from *Religious Education*, (ed.) Dom Phillip Jebb, London 1968, ch. 8, p. 165.

14. Quoted in F. R. Barry, *Christian Ethics and Secular Society*, London 1966, p. 147.

15. F. A. Olafson, 'Teaching About Religion: Some Reservations', *Harvard Educational Review*, 1967, p. 240.

16. *The Times*, 30 November 1968.

17. M. L. W. Laistner, *Christianity and Pagan Culture*, New York 1961, p. 51.

18. F. R. Barry, *Christian Ethics and Secular Society*, London 1966, p. 154.

19. Daniel Jenkins, *Beyond Religion*, London 1962, p. 23.

For Further Reading

Chapter 1

Horace Bushnell, *Christian Nurture*, Yale University Press, 1966.

J. Donald Butler, *Religious Education: The Foundations and Practice of Nurture*, Harper & Row, 1962.

R. S. Lee, *Your Growing Child and Religion*, Pelican Books, 1965.

Chapter 2

Ian A. Muirhead, *Education in the New Testament*, Monographs in Christian Education, Association Press, 1965.

Lewis J. Sherrill, *The Rise of Christian Education*, The Macmillan Company, 1960.

Josef A. Jungmann, *Handing on the Faith: A Manual of Catechetics*, Burns & Oates, 1959.

Chapter 3

Sara Little, *The Role of the Bible in Contemporary Christian Education*, John Knox Press, 1961.

J. Stanley Glen, *The Recovery of the Teaching Ministry*, Westminster Press, 1960.

Ronald Goldman, *Readiness for Religion: A Basis for Developmental Religious Education*, Routledge and Kegan Paul, 1965.

123

Chapter 4

Douglas Rhymes, *Prayer in the Secular City*, Lutterworth Press, 1967.

Iris V. Cully, *Christian Worship and Church Education*, Westminster Press, 1967.

John G. Williams, *Worship and the Modern Child*, SPCK, 1962.

Chapter 5

Karl Barth, *Church Dogmatics*, III, 4 (Parents and Children), T. & T. Clark, 1961.

C. Ellis Nelson, *Where Faith Begins*, John Knox Press, 1967.

John Wilson (ed.), *Introduction to Moral Education*, Penguin Books, 1967.

Chapter 6

F. H. Hilliard (ed.), *Christianity in Education*, Hibbert Lectures, Allen and Unwin, 1966.

Bernard Tucker (ed.), *Catholic Education in a Secular Society*, Sheed and Ward, 1968.

John C. Bennett, *Christians and the State*, Charles Scribner's Sons, 1958 (see especially chapter XVI).

Index of Names

125

Baptism of infants we fail when we do no more. 21.

Sunday worship is dull for y. people. 33.

R.I. has to answer question which children
have not yet asked. 56.